CONSULTING THE COINS

*A New Age Interpretation
of the I Ching*

CONSULTING THE COINS

A New Age Interpretation of the I Ching

PETER HAZEL

LOTHIAN PUBLISHING COMPANY PTY LTD
MELBOURNE SYDNEY AUCKLAND

A Lothian book

LOTHIAN PUBLISHING COMPANY PTY. LTD.
11 Munro Street, Port Melbourne, Victoria 3207

Copyright © Peter Hazel 1990
First published 1990

National Library of Australia
Cataloguing-in-publication data:

Hazel, Peter, 1947–
    Consulting the coins: a New Age interpretation
    of the I ching.
    ISBN 0 85091 406 X.
    1. I ching. 2. Divination. I. Title.
133.33

Cover design by David Constable
Text designed by Mark Davis
Typeset in Sabon and Copperplate Gothic by Meredith
    Typesetting, Melbourne
Printed by Australian Print Group

CONTENTS

In memory of my father, James Hazel

The *Book of Changes* is also the book of freedom
for without change no choice would be possible and
without choice there could be no freedom.

INTRODUCTION

The *I Ching*, or *Book of Changes*, is said to be the oldest book in the world, and has a spirit of its own. It is an artefact from a remarkable period of human evolution, the ancient civilisation of China, which emerged about 6000 years ago. This civilisation did not just appear in 4000 BC: its development would have taken many centuries. Therefore, the pedigree of the *I Ching* is impeccable: a document from the dawn of civilisation. Yet the ancient Chinese were not very different from us. They paid taxes and were subject to an elaborate and extensive bureaucracy. They had police, crime and bankruptcy. They fell in love, got involved in lawsuits and, in short, knew all the joys and troubles with which we are familiar. They had the same emotions, pleasures and griefs, went to weddings and funerals, and experienced economic plenty and depression.

Like our own society, life then had glaring faults. People often felt the need to consult an oracle. The *I Ching* emerged as a book of divination and a source of Confucian and Taoist philosophy. The work is based on the simple principle that the universe exists because of a tension between opposites: yin and yang, male and female, day and night, being and non-being. Furthermore, the universe is circular in form and motion, to which everything is subject. All things undergo change and, consequently, endure the pangs of birth, growth, maturity, decay and death. Everything, from a galaxy to a mountain to a man to a worm, is subject to this cycle.

The one thing that never changes is change itself, a concept that has always intrigued humankind. The whole of life is one process of endless internal and external change. The *I Ching* is a sociological work that attempts to systematise and explain this process. It sees humans as being part of the natural process of cyclical change. This law operates in nature and applies in the same way to humans.

The *I Ching* recognises three kinds of change:

1   *Non-change*: This is the very slow-moving background against which all change is obvious. This sort of change usually applies to what we usually call the status quo, and is represented by the broad cycles of birth and death, which take an average of 70 or 80 years to become complete.

2   *Cyclic change*: This form of change is generally the most predictable, and includes the day, the lunar months, the seasons, the round of daily life, and also, to a certain extent, the cycle of birth and death.

3   *Consequential change*: This is straightforward action and reaction; changes that occur due to a specific stimulus. Events occur when forced: they may be predicted because events move according to a very simple rule — as water flows downhill, events *always* follow the *path of least resistance*. The main difficulty lies in discovering just where this path lies, and what constitutes the path of least resistance.

An examination of your life, and that of your society, should allow you to recognise how these types of change affect you. Interestingly, there is an entrenched opposition to accepting the simple view that things change because it is in their nature to change. Yet, even now, late in the 20th century, most of us fear change. Part of the reason is probably an obsession with security. Change is generally regarded as negative — something to be avoided and delayed. Change is not only inevitable, but it is also life-enhancing, healthy and fascinating. Resistance to change makes change difficult and the result is often painful.

The *I Ching* was written to help individuals and societies adjust to, and accept, change. The authorship of the book is obscure but seems to be the result of many years of study by several eminent sages and scholars. They analysed the workings of the universe and distilled their observations into sets of hexagrams based on binary code, expressed as broken and unbroken lines, which represent the tension of opposites. This group of lines may be combined into 64 different patterns. From variations of the individual lines within these 64 hexagrams, a further 4096 possibilities are explored.

Each of the 64 hexagrams is a scenario, which, when put together, represent all the major situations common to humankind. The *I Ching* purports to be no less than a complete manual of life. On one level it is a straightforward oracle, which you may consult by asking questions pertaining to your love life or your business affairs. On another level the *I Ching* is a manual of illumination, which instructs those seeking spiritual enlightenment.

I may be guilty of the worst kind of intellectual arrogance to attempt to rewrite a classic like the *I Ching*. However, the original authors of this work are very far removed from us in space and time, and their imagery is often unfamiliar to us. My interpretation is a humble attempt to transform the eternal expressions and concepts of change and life contained in the *I Ching* into a modern equivalent.

I would urge all interested readers to refer to other interpretations of the *I Ching*. Most useful among these are the translation by Richard Wilhelm (Routledge and Kegan Paul, London, 1983) and the translation by Legge (Signet Books, New York, 1971).

CONSULTING THE *BOOK OF CHANGES* USING THE COIN METHOD

The coin method is the most simple and direct way to consult the *I Ching*.

It is best to approach the *I Ching* in a serious frame of mind. Systems like the *I Ching* and the tarot work like computers: when the input is rubbish the output is also rubbish. That is to say, if your approach is frivolous, the answer will certainly be frivolous. The *I Ching* states clearly that if one approaches it with the 'sincerity' necessary, an answer will be given. (See Hexagram 4, 'Youthful Inexperience', in the Wilhelm translation of the *I Ching*.) Only a serious-minded approach will answer your purpose.

Some people like to make a small ritual of a consultation. You might light a stick of incense, carefully lay out the materials, which are used for no other purpose than consulting the *I Ching*. You might do some deep breathing, or use other techniques to concentrate the mind. Such approaches are not strictly necessary, but they do seem to help.

You will need: *three coins* These may be any three coins. It is possible to buy old Chinese copper 'cash' coins, which are small, round bronze or copper coins with a square hole in the centre, usually with Chinese characters in relief. Otherwise, use three coins of uniform size, coins that you can put away and use for no other purpose than consulting the *I Ching*. Some people like to use old silver coins, like silver threepences or sixpences. Having chosen your coins, you must now ascribe a value to them: 2 to one side, 3 to the other. Personally, I count heads as 2, and tails as 3. You can do it the other way around if you so wish, but once you have decided you must be consistent, and forever after stick to the values you have ascribed or your readings will be inconsistent and unreliable.

A *notebook* It is useful to create a permanent record of your consultations. I always date my readings, and make a brief note of the question asked.

THE METHOD

The coins must be cast a total of six times. Because they have a value of 2 for one side, and 3 for the other, the casts can yield four possible totals: 6, 7, 8 or 9. You will use these numbers to build up your hexagrams in the following manner:

6 is a moving line. It changes, from broken −X− to unbroken ——. Moving lines represent the changing elements in your situation, and add detail to the consultation.

7 is a non-moving line. It is an unbroken line ——.

8 is a non-moving line. It is a broken line − −.

9 is a moving line. It changes, from unbroken −θ− to broken − −.

The moving lines allow for the construction of a second hexagram.

The first hexagram is regarded as representing the present moment, or the immediate past. The second hexagram is regarded as representing the most probable outcome of the situation outlined in the first hexagram: the future.

The following is an example of a cast of the coins. Imagine that you have just cast the coins six times, and obtained the numbers 7, 8, 6, 7, 9, 6. Here is how you construct your hexagrams:

Hexagrams must be constructed from the *bottom up*. Therefore, our throw of 7, 8, 6, 7, 9, 6, following the rules about moving and unmoving lines, is written:

6 (Moving line)	−X−	changes to	——
9 (Moving line)	−θ−	changes to	− −
7 Unbroken line	——	remains	——

6 (Moving line)	−X−	changes to	——
8 Broken line	– –	remains	– –
7 Unbroken line	——	remains	——

The next step is to turn to the Key on page 9, in order to find out the number of your hexagrams. To do this, look up the trigram of the top, which is:

Then look up the trigram on the bottom, which is:

Now find the number in the box where these two trigrams intersect. In this case, it is hexagram 17. Repeat this process to find the number of the second hexagram, which happens to be hexagram 30. You now have two hexagrams to consider. Besides reading the Scenario, Business Implications, Love Implications, and Spiritual Implications in hexagram 17, you should also read the additional notes for six in the third place, nine in the fifth place, and six at the top. These moving lines represent the changing elements within your situation, and lead on to the second hexagram, which shows the most probable outcome of the changes, provided you follow the *I Ching's* instructions.

This simple method is fairly easy to master and you should be able to consult the coins with great confidence after a few practice runs.

WHAT SORT OF QUESTIONS MAY YOU ASK?

General questions are the best. Obviously, the *I Ching* is not going to respond to a question regarding next week's winning Gold Lotto numbers, or which horse will win the Melbourne Cup. This does not mean you cannot be specific: you can ask such questions as 'what is the outcome if I marry a particular person?' or 'what will be the outcome of this business venture?' and get a comprehensible answer. There is, of course, always the danger that you will not particularly like the answer you get, but that's a risk you run when consulting any oracle.

If you don't like the answer you get, you can always carry on casting the coins until a favourable reply surfaces. Naturally, such a method is ridiculous. Repeated consultations, that is, more than one or at the most two throws per question, is bound to result in nonsense. When consulting the *I Ching*, or any oracle for that matter, the law of diminishing returns definitely applies.

Some people reserve the *I Ching* for the most important questions which arise in their lives, such as when they are at a 'crossroads' facing a decision that will have a major effect on their future.

How you use the *I Ching* is entirely up to you, but the above comments may help you to make the best possible use of the oracle. Practice will make you familiar with what sort of questions you may ask and reasonably expect to have answered.

WHY DOES IT WORK?

You are the centre of the universe — the centre, that is, as far as you are concerned, so when you cast the coins or the bones, do a tarot layout, or study the entrails of a carefully selected and freshly slaughtered sacrificial beast, the randomly achieved answer is, in a real way, representative of the state of the cosmos as it pertains to you at the moment of consultation. But remember, the answers must be read and understood through the questions you have asked. Sometimes, the answers will seem to have little or no relevance to the question you asked. The *I Ching* is tricky that way: it seems that sometimes it answers questions you didn't ask, which relate to questions or problems you are subconsciously concerned with.

Any answer you arrive at should be regarded as a guide, a scenario that might help you to make a decision. No matter how much faith you have in the *I Ching* — or any other oracle for that matter — it can only point, only advise in fairly broad terms. The final decision is always yours. The most important thing you bring to a consultation with the *I Ching* is your intuition. Ultimately, it is your own feelings that will decide matters.

THE KEY

Lower Trigrams \ Upper Trigrams	Heaven	Thunder	Rain	Mountain	Earth	Wind	Fire	Lake
Heaven	1	34	5	26	11	9	14	43
Thunder	25	51	3	27	24	42	21	17
Rain	6	40	29	4	7	59	64	47
Mountain	33	62	39	52	15	53	56	31
Earth	12	16	8	23	2	20	35	45
Wind	44	32	48	18	46	57	50	28
Fire	13	55	63	22	36	37	30	49
Lake	10	54	60	41	19	61	38	58

The Hexagrams

1

HEAVEN, THE ACTIVE AND CREATIVE

THE SCENARIO Your situation is imbued with primal power. Present is the energy that motivates. It is time to plant, for all that you plant now will grow and bear fruit. All effort directed towards worthwhile goals will meet with success. Your situation may be likened to a blank page waiting to be written on, needing only your response to achieve creative potential. All you need to do is work steadily and exert your will to bring about your desires.

The wise person consciously seeks to strengthen and improve the inner self and the situation by avoiding and rejecting all inferior and degrading elements that might exist in or enter into the personality or the situation.

BUSINESS IMPLICATIONS It is now possible to begin a great project, to launch a new product, to take calculated risks. All reasonable endeavours undertaken now will certainly succeed.

LOVE IMPLICATIONS If you were asking about a particular person when you threw this hexagram you can proceed in creating a relationship with every confidence, for this is a worthy person, someone you can trust. You can marry, and with honesty and goodwill on your part, create a successful, warm, honest, loving and long-lasting partnership.

SPIRITUAL IMPLICATIONS This is a powerful spiritual hexagram that represents the primal creative force that permeates the entire cosmos. This is the stillness against which all movement in the universe is contrasted. You should consciously seek to improve your spiritual self and situation by avoiding and rejecting all inferior and degrading elements that might exist in or threaten to enter into your situation or your personality.

THE MOVING ELEMENTS IN THE SITUATION

Nine at the beginning: It is not yet time to act. Your talents have not yet been recognised. Be patient; be true to your goals and aims. Do not waste energy trying to force matters before the time is ripe. Bide your time and success must come.

Nine in the second place: This is the beginning of activity. You have chosen the field in which you will make a mark. You stand out because of your evident sense of purpose and reliability. You are destined to succeed.

Nine in the third place: Success carries with it many dangers. Ambition can destroy your integrity. Praise can corrode your ability. Do not allow your considerable potential to be restricted by the narrow reality of success and its trappings. If you can avoid the pitfalls that now lie before you, your success can be great.

Nine in the fourth place: You are at a crossroads. You must choose between the high path and the low. You may either devote yourself to worldly affairs — becoming 'important', wealthy and great — or you may withdraw from the world and direct your energies to spiritual development. It is important to choose according to your true inclinations.

Nine in the fifth place: Great success is indicated. Your influence will be widespread because you are in the right place at the right time, and there is harmony.

Nine at the top: A warning: your ambition exceeds your abilities. Pride comes before a fall: you are too arrogant. You consider yourself to be above the masses. This leads to isolation. You lose touch, and this leads to failure.

2

EARTH, THE RECEPTIVE

THE SCENARIO This hexagram symbolises the magic fertility of the female. It represents a simple flow of energy that is unjudging, unquestioning, and accepting. It is a creative yielding. This is not a time to force matters but to roll with the flow; a time to incubate new ideas, to be pregnant with fruitful creations rather than to be actively, forcefully busy with affairs. At this time you are a medium, a tube as it were, through which events and activities flow. You should behave like a thoroughbred mare: docile, mild and yet strong. Carry out whatever duties are yours — as father, mother, husband, wife, employee, son or daughter — with devotion and moral force.

BUSINESS IMPLICATIONS This is not a time to be aggressive in the marketplace but, rather, a time for the careful gestation and development of new products and strategies. Partnerships can be very fruitful now, and mergers are likely to succeed. Concentrate on research, reorganisation and development. Faction fights and splits within the organisation must be avoided at all costs. Do not try to acquire or maintain a commanding position. This is a good time to call in expert advice.

LOVE IMPLICATIONS Now is the time to co-operate and be devoted, patient and loyal. If you try to force matters you will regret it. Roll with the flow, and don't be bossy. If you are truly in love, you are no longer entirely independent, so don't try to pretend otherwise.

SPIRITUAL IMPLICATIONS Receive without having chosen anything; give without the active desire to be benevolent. Be a creative receptacle. It is not your task to lead, but to follow and be of assistance. Support the world and those around you with moral strength and excellence. Allow yourself to be guided.

THE MOVING ELEMENTS IN THE SITUATION

Six at the beginning: The signs of the inevitable decay of your current situation have begun to appear. Make preparations for the deterioration of what you now have, for decay will increase until dissolution takes place. It is possible to delay this process by recognising the signs when they first appear and countering them; but decay is inevitable.

Six in the second place: Accommodate yourself to the events occurring around you. Accept what comes and adapt yourself accordingly. Artifice or special intentions are inappropriate to the situation: only receptive adaptability will avail you now.

Six in the third place: Avoid fame and recognition, for these will interfere with the naturally slow maturation of your true abilities. Act not for personal glorification but, rather, for the good of others, or to further an ideal.

Six in the fourth place: Recognition or success will cause enemies to appear. You must be reticent and reserved. Do not under any circumstances put yourself forward or challenge the status quo.

Six in the fifth place: Success depends on your discretion. You must be refined, discreet and modest. Restrain aggression and egotistic desires now. Do not brag or complain, but let your actions speak for themselves, showing your quality indirectly.

Six at the top: There is an indication that you are not entitled to the position you occupy, and this will inevitably bring you into conflict with others who have a claim to what you see as yours. You are trying to rule when you should be serving. This conflict will be very injurious to all parties involved.

3

PROBLEMS OR DIFFICULTIES IN THE BEGINNING

THE SCENARIO This hexagram is symbolised by a young blade of grass struggling to emerge against some obstacle or barrier. It is a time of growth — when an idea or situation struggles to obtain material form and organisation. It is therefore a time of growth and opportunity.

Disorder waits to be ordered. Haste is wasted, as the situation is subject to the time limitations of natural growth. Nothing must be forced and patience is urged: any premature action can cause failure.

Concern yourself with the basic principles and ethics of the situation. If matters are not managed properly now when they are still in formation, the possibility of later problems may be overlooked. You must persevere. Make whatever compromises are necessary and, above all, do not give up or allow the situation to stagnate, for that will create difficulties. Your job is simply to bring organisation to chaos. It might help to seek expert advice.

BUSINESS IMPLICATIONS It is not a time to take important or major steps, as a basic disorder exists within your organisation that must be addressed before you attempt anything else. There are disputes and disagreements, and business is poor. This disorder must be remedied before there is any chance of positive growth. You must clarify the principles, aims and policies of your organisation. Above all, be aware that you are now faced with one of two major possibilities: the opportunity for growth that a thorough reorganisation can accomplish, or the inevitable decline and decay caused by disorganisation.

LOVE IMPLICATIONS From the very beginning there is something amiss that is hindering romance, or you are experiencing difficulties that may be traced to the roots of your relationship. Your relationship faces a struggle to obtain form and organisation, and disorder and disagreement plague the parties involved. For the affair to succeed, you must persevere and not hesitate to compromise. Haste is out of the question; only patience and careful exploration of the possibilities can succeed.

SPIRITUAL IMPLICATIONS You are at the beginning of the spiritual path, which is characterised by difficulty or chaos. However, you must realise that just as chaos lies at the heart of order, so order is implicit at the heart of chaos. You must take great care in choosing the sort of organisation you will use to shape your spiritual life. Keep in mind the disastrous mistakes that can be made at the very beginning of any enterprise. Do not be ashamed to seek help or advice.

THE MOVING ELEMENTS IN THE SITUATION

Nine at the beginning: You are faced with a confusing obstacle at the very beginning of your enterprise. Do not attempt to force matters or push on regardless. You must realise that you need expert assistance and advice. Seek these in a humble spirit, avoiding arrogance, and the right people will be attracted to you.

Six in the second place: Confusion and difficulty are upon you. You feel beset, and suddenly an offer of some sort of assistance is made. It must be refused, however, because it comes from an unexpected, unrelated and possibly unacceptable quarter. Acceptance may well entail onerous obligations that will impair your freedom to make decisions. It may be better to bide your time until a return to more normal conditions.

Six in the third place: You are in difficulties and in grave danger of failure and disgrace. You have no reliable guidance in the situation. It is wiser to withdraw from a no-win situation than to try to force matters.

Six in the fourth place: You are in a difficult position. You must recognise that you lack the power to be independent. An opportunity to make an influential connection will soon arise. You will need to make the necessary overture, but do not allow false pride to hinder you — ask for help without hesitation, and all will go well.

Nine in the fifth place: Unfortunately, you are in a position where you will be misunderstood. People will actively work against you, distorting your intentions and efforts. You must not attempt to undertake any great endeavour. Lie low and work unobtrusively and consciously until the situation improves and problems disappear.

Six at the top: The difficulties here are too great to overcome. You have lost all sense of perspective, and you feel swamped by difficulties. You are inclined to give up and wallow in self-pity, but it would be more positive to stop indulging yourself in this way and look in other directions.

4

YOUTHFUL INEXPERIENCE OR FOLLY, IGNORANCE

THE SCENARIO This is the hexagram of education in progress. You must understand that it is necessary to admit your ignorance: only by accepting the fact that you know very little can you begin to learn. Your ignorance is the result of inexperience. You have much to learn and it is time you began to ask the right questions. Your luck is good, and the situation represents an excellent opportunity for personal growth.

You must recognise your ignorance and the need to seek out a teacher or some source of knowledge. This requires modesty and respectful interest, without which you won't learn anything. Furthermore, learning requires perseverance, for lessons are learned point by point and character is developed by gradual, thorough cultivation.

Go forward confident that failure through inexperience or youthful impetuosity is usually a valuable learning experience and that, in any case, your efforts will often be successful. But don't forget: young fools often need discipline.

BUSINESS IMPLICATIONS Inexperience, which amounts to confusion, is operating here. You need to investigate training methods or perhaps the hiring of mature expertise. However, members of your staff will learn a great deal from their mistakes: development is at work and, if you are prepared to wait, inexperience will eventually become expertise.

LOVE IMPLICATIONS You are young, inexperienced and in love. There will be much gaucheness and many mistakes and misunderstandings but, given goodwill on both sides, the lessons will be learned, for both luck and love are in your favour.

SPIRITUAL IMPLICATIONS You need to cultivate the humility of the seeker. There is much you do not know. Seek out a guide, master or guru. Do this with modesty, humility, respectful acceptance, and an awareness of your inexperience. You need to know that you just don't know.

THE MOVING ELEMENTS IN THE SITUATION

Six at the beginning: Youthful inexperience is playful and not particularly inclined to take matters seriously. A degree of discipline is necessary, yet care should be taken not to impose excessive restrictions, for this will hinder creative development. Discipline should not be allowed to degenerate into mere drill, which numbs the soul, humiliates and, ultimately, restricts.

Nine in the second place: Learn how to treat with compassion, forbearance and wisdom the shortcomings and foibles of others. Cultivate a kindly tolerance towards the follies of humankind.

Six in the third place: You are in grave danger of making a major mistake. You are about to throw yourself into situations that you cannot control, attempting the unachievable, slavishly imitating a strong personality or influence, and losing your individuality. The image is of a young inexperienced woman who throws herself at any available strong man when she owes it to her dignity to wait until she is wooed.

Six in the fourth place: You truly are a youthful fool, an unrealistic know-all lost in fantasy. The coming rude awakening and humiliation may teach you something. You are not humble enough: painful experience is your only effective teacher.

Six in the fifth place: You are inexperienced, yet have the correct attitude. You are not arrogant and you seek knowledge in an innocent, non-presumptuous and unpretentious manner. This means that you are able to accept advice and so begin to learn.

Nine at the top: You are an incorrigible fool whose behaviour is not conducive to education. A good shake-up is needed. This may apply to a fool with whom you are dealing, in which case penalties must not be imposed in a spirit of revenge or anger. The idea is to curb foolish excess. Punishment can help 'cure' your inexperience and prevent transgressions that may harm others.

5

WAITING: CALCULATED INACTIVITY, PATIENT ANTICIPATION

THE SCENARIO   This can be a difficult time that is not really under your control. There is a lack of an obvious course of action. You probably feel restless and have a strong need to act, yet there is no clear way.

   You must tread water and be patient. If you flounder or try to force matters, you will regret it. A considerable difficulty or obstacle is hindering action. Your only option is to bide your time until things begin to go your way. There is absolutely no use in worrying or trying to shape the future until the right time for action occurs. Be detached, and eat and drink in comfort and contentment. Answer the bleating of critics with silence.

BUSINESS IMPLICATIONS   This is a time to hold still and consolidate. You must realise that you have very little control over events at the moment. A big problem hinders everything, and calculated inactivity is the best course. The time for firm and decisive action will come, and you will be ready to act, provided that you are able to face the situation without self-deception or hopeful illusions.

LOVE IMPLICATIONS   There is not a great deal happening within the relationship, but you must not worry. There are elements in the situation that are beyond your control; therefore, action, accusation or any sort of emotional push is useless and even counterproductive. This is a time for patience. Bide your time and wait for things to swing your way. Meanwhile, enjoy what you have without making demands.

SPIRITUAL IMPLICATIONS The path is not apparent. Curb your impatience and fortify yourself with food and drink. Cultivate patience, for a path will appear like a light breaking through the fog of illusion and self-deception. By cultivating patience, and unflinching self-honesty, you can prepare yourself to recognise this path.

THE MOVING ELEMENTS IN THE SITUATION

Nine at the beginning: Everything seems to be fine, yet you are troubled by worries about the future — you harbour a feeling that something is about to go wrong. Simply carry on with your normal life, for worry is only a drain on your strength. You must never allow the possibility of future problems to weigh you down: after all, nothing may happen.

Nine in the second place: Problems are developing and there is a tendency to lay blame, but try to stay calm. You may be the subject of gossip, which you must ignore, for slander and rumour are best answered by dignified silence.

Nine in the third place: Something or someone has tempted you to act prematurely. Unfortunately, this has placed you in a position of weakness, which exposes you to attack by elements that will take advantage of your condition. All you can do is realise the seriousness of the situation and exercise caution.

Six in the fourth place: The situation is extremely serious: a matter of life and death. Circumstances are completely beyond your control. You cannot advance or retreat — all you can do is stand fast, be strong and take what comes as best you can. As soon as any avenue of escape appears, you must seize upon it.

Nine in the fifth place: It is time for recreation. Here is an interval of peace that will allow you to gain a sense of perspective. It is important to enjoy this moment of leisure without forgetting that there is a job ahead, a task to be accomplished. You will work better for having taken a break.

Six at the top: The waiting is over; everything seems to be going wrong and all your work seems to have been in vain. You are in deep trouble, but help is at hand provided you can recognise and accept it. Just at the darkest moment there will be an unexpected reprieve, an outside intervention that may initially seem alarming, but you should understand that good fortune often arrives in disguise. Treat this unexpected turn of events with respect and acceptance.

6

CONFLICT

THE SCENARIO Here is a situation of tension. Outright conflict is almost certain no matter how careful you are. There are conflicting opposites here; you may well feel that you are in the right, but you are asking for trouble if you insist on having your own way or push ahead with your point of view. You are advised to. separate yourself from the influence of any opposition. If this is not possible, a cautious compromise may be the only way. If you employ cunning or aggression you will only force a struggle and bring down upon yourself all the dangers inherent in conflict situations.

If conflict is inevitable you must do all you can to calm the situation and avoid its escalation. Seek arbitration if possible.

Generally, conflict between people may be solved by separating the contending parties. Your own inner conflict may be solved by distracting your attention to other matters.

BUSINESS IMPLICATIONS To avoid conflict in business ensure that the rights and duties of staff are exactly defined. When assessing a product or a market, aim to recognise areas where competition and conflict can arise, so these possibilities can be adequately planned for.

LOVE IMPLICATIONS The two of you are incompatible. The problems your relationship faces can be solved only by separation. You are entangled in conflict that will only escalate. The relationship will end in bitterness if you persist. You may try compromise, but you are so fundamentally incompatible that no matter how careful you are, there will always be conflict.

SPIRITUAL IMPLICATIONS An inner conflict is obstructing your progress and must be sidestepped as it is unsolvable. It is necessary to simply drop this conflict, whatever it may be, and direct your full attention to other matters. Some problems are best solved by ignoring them for, due to their illusory nature, they tend to vanish when they are disregarded.

THE MOVING ELEMENTS IN THE SITUATION

Six at the beginning: Potential conflict is in the air and the best thing to do is simply dismiss it. You may feel victimised, but this feeling should be ignored. Things will go your way in the end.

Nine in the second place: You are in conflict with someone who is very powerful and much too strong for you. You should retreat. If you permit false pride or obstinacy to propel you into conflict, you will be badly beaten.

Six in the third place: You are in a position to avoid conflict provided you are willing to settle for the status quo. Do not be ostentatious or try to own too much, because you will attract enemies. Be a quiet achiever, get the job done, and do not squabble over the credit or the glory. It isn't worth it.

Nine in the fourth place: You are discontent with your situation or position and imagine that matters might be improved by provoking a conflict with someone. You may well be very tempted because your opponent is weaker so victory seems certain. But you must restrain yourself. Retain your dignity and cultivate your sense of inner worth and peace. Only this can bring good fortune.

Nine in the fifth place: Seek arbitration from an impartial authority whose power is sufficient to settle the dispute. You will win if you are in the right.

Nine at the top: You have insisted on pursuing a conflict to the bitter end. You may feel that victory is possible, and even within your grasp. This is an illusion. Your enemy will never surrender, and you face an endless conflict in which resolution or victory is impossible.

7

THE ARMY, GROUP OR COLLECTIVE ACTION

THE SCENARIO Many occurrences at this time have a single cause or controlling factor. You must discover what this factor is. This is a hexagram of preparation: you are about to undertake a great task, or involve yourself in a conflict. Ceaseless action and a strong leader are necessary.

If you are the leader to emerge during this time of need, you must lead not by force, but by education, generosity and leniency. Violence should always be seen as a last resort, to be used only when all other options have failed. You must explain to members of the group what action is required from them, for people need an aim to which they can consciously pledge themselves. This approach is the only way you can achieve the unity and strength of purpose necessary for your undertaking. Without this, achievement or victory is impossible.

BUSINESS IMPLICATIONS You will gain nothing if your staff is not behind you. You must motivate your people by giving them clear objectives. There would be advantage in giving them a stake in the success of the firm: they would work harder and be more co-operative and willing. Only workers who share in the profits of their labour can be relied upon to work at their optimum in all conditions.

LOVE IMPLICATIONS This is not a relationship between equals: you may be the weaker or the stronger but, either way, making this relationship work will take a great deal of effort. One of you must be a follower who offers all possible support. The other must be a competent leader who is willing and able to take on a dominant role. The dominant personality must be generous, involved, patient and forgiving. Is that you?

SPIRITUAL IMPLICATIONS You must organise your spiritual search as if you were an army preparing for war. You must have a clear objective, then mobilise all your forces to achieve it. Let all your activity stem from a single cause: your aim for enlightenment.

THE MOVING ELEMENTS IN THE SITUATION:

Six at the beginning: When you start something it is vital to be properly organised. You need valid aims and objectives, and your helpers need to be well organised. Disorganisation will result in failure.

Nine in the second place: It is important that good communication is maintained in all undertakings, so that a finger can be kept on the pulse. You must share the good and the bad with your helpers. Success often hinges on the quality and efficiency of your lines of communication.

Six in the third place: This line suggests an absence of vision and deficient leadership: both will soon attract misfortune.

Six in the fourth place: You are faced with a superior enemy or an unsolvable problem. The only option is to retreat. You cannot win in the present circumstances, and orderly withdrawal is your only viable alternative.

Six in the fifth place: An element of chaos that is comparable to an invasion by a hostile army has entered the situation. Chaos must be avoided at all costs. Maintain discipline and seek experienced guidance. Above all, the coherence of the group and the co-ordination of effort must be maintained.

Six at the top: Once the objective of the group has been achieved, it is important that everyone shares in the profits. These may consist of goods and money, or power and position. Special care must be taken in the delegation of power. Inferior people may be satisfied with money, while power and position should be reserved for those morally and spiritually suited to high position.

8

UNION, JOINING THE DIVERSE

THE SCENARIO This is an interesting and challenging situation of great potential. It represents civilisation, or the need that exists in humans to be joined together. You must recognise that we need to complement each other. Now is a very good time to get involved, join something, stand for office, or marry.

If you feel you are divided within yourself, you should consult expert help or advice. You require a sense of social responsibility, purpose, and virtue. If you lack these, you will create confusion and chaos around you. In fact, you should consult the *I Ching* again to check whether you possess the necessary qualities of grace, constancy and perseverance to make the present situation successful. You need, also, to act quickly: procrastination can ruin everything.

You will find that co-operation with others will overcome obstacles; therefore, be sure to organise co-operation with others. Spread wide the wings of your perception, for human society is held together through a wide community of interests that allows people to be individuals. The union of the diverse takes place because things tend to complement each other.

BUSINESS IMPLICATIONS Here is a situation requiring you to merge with others of like mind, so that you or your company becomes part of an organic fellowship. Obstacles in the marketplace, or in the production area, may be over-

come by co-operation and an understanding of the whole-
ness and interrelation of buyers and sellers. This may be
difficult because of the nature of competition, which can
be destructive and expensive. If the merger does not eventuate the result will be isolation and failure.

LOVE IMPLICATIONS Your relationship may be in some
difficulty. You need to acquire a sense of responsibility,
purpose, and virtue in order to save it. You are advised to
consult the coins again to ask whether you are possessed
of the qualities necessary to make the union work.

SPIRITUAL IMPLICATIONS Union with like-minded
people is now necessary. Isolation is not serving your purpose. Your selfishness has become an obstacle.

THE MOVING ELEMENTS IN THE SITUATION

Six at the beginning: You need to recognise that sincerity is the
proper basis on which relationships are built. You must
simply be yourself; be honest and unaffected. This will
attract unexpected good fortune.

Six in the second place: If you act the part of the obsequious office
seeker, looking to gain advantage for yourself from your
association with others, you will not achieve much advantage. Do not seek the approval of others; trust yourself.
Don't lose your dignity by being servile.

Six in the third place: You have fallen in with the wrong crowd.
Your reputation is in danger. By identifying yourself and
being too intimate with the wrong people you will inhibit
your chances of connecting with the right people on other
occasions.

Six in the fourth place: You are in a supporting role in a relationship
or union. Be constant and openly show your support.

Nine in the fifth place: You can trust fate at this particular time.
You will meet the right people. There will be a voluntary
dependence between those involved in this union. There
should be much freedom to come and go and to express
opinions and ideas.

Six at the top: The moment for unity has passed. In fact, there was
something fundamentally wrong with the situation from
the very start. You are advised to direct your attention
elsewhere.

9

THE POWER OF THE WEAK

THE SCENARIO Something powerful is being held in check by a small weakness. Your plans are being delayed by an unknown, possibly external factor. This is an unfulfilling situation about which you can do little. No option will be effectual, but remember that this is a temporary situation. To expect more than what is possible now will lead to disappointment and the devaluation of what you have. There is almost nothing you can do to alleviate matters, except in very small ways. Attend to quality in all your relationships and work, and wait patiently for the time to change. Do not be tempted to use brute force, as you will regret it.

BUSINESS IMPLICATIONS A big idea or enterprise is delayed, and there is almost nothing you can do about it. Only gentleness and patience will see you through this temporary slump. You will look back on this time as an unprofitable and luckless period.

LOVE IMPLICATIONS There is something wrong, and things are simply not developing the way you'd hoped. However, things may go your way later if you are patient and gentle.

SPIRITUAL IMPLICATIONS You are suffering from one of the many routine blockages that can affect the anchorite or the traveller on the spiritual path. You may be disappointed by the seeming slowness of your progress. You should now only attempt to refine your nature, mind and behaviour in small ways. Nothing great should be expected or attempted.

THE MOVING ELEMENTS IN THE SITUATION

Nine at the beginning: You are tempted to press forward and sweep obstacles out of the way. But if you use force you will only encounter more obstacles. It is better to hold back at this time, for in the nature of things it is wise and reasonable not to make gains by force.

Nine in the second place: The way is blocked. Your only reasonable action is to retreat and wait patiently until the situation changes.

Nine in the third place: Here you have attempted to force matters and push forward because victory seems possible. The opposition or problem seems slight, but power lies with the side that appears weak. External events will hinder your advance and you are bound to fail.

Six in the fourth place: You are in a difficult and even dangerous situation. Your only option is to be completely honest and sincere. Only the power of disinterested truth can prevail.

Nine in the fifth place: You must share your wealth and influence. You need to be in a partnership, a relationship of mutual reinforcement. True wealth is that which is shared rather than hoarded.

Nine at the top: Success, which is very close, has been achieved by sheer perseverance. In fact, you've won a battle. Now you must stop, rest and consolidate. You will only regret it if you press on. Stop and wait until it is time to move again.

10

≡≡≡
≡ ≡
≡≡≡

CONDUCT, BEHAVIOUR

THE SCENARIO You are in a situation of difficulty and danger: you may be dealing with wild and intractable people. However, you must remember that pleasant manners succeed even with irritable people, so correct conduct will allow you to obtain your goal even in difficult circumstances. Therefore, pay close attention to your personal conduct. Base all your interactions with others on what you consider to be their inner worth, rather than on their external rank. At all times you must retain good humour, impeccable manners and composure.

This situation allows you to take a chance or risk that pays off. The situation is likened to someone who treads on the tail of a tiger but is not bitten.

BUSINESS IMPLICATIONS You are taking a chance, and you are up against a powerful opponent. This opposition might easily crush you, but you will manage to pull off a coup, provided you are good humoured, composed and well mannered. Personal style will be the reason for success — nothing else will do. Be careful that, in regard to promotion and recognition within your business, differences in rank are not arbitrary but, rather, based on merit or the inner qualities of your employees.

LOVE IMPLICATIONS You are going to take a chance. Be careful to discriminate between the inferior and the superior elements in your situation. Good manners will get you where you want to be.

SPIRITUAL IMPLICATIONS Ensure that your outer personality conforms to the qualities of your inner self. When dealing with others be careful to react to their true selves, and not merely to their apparent social rank.

THE MOVING ELEMENTS IN THE SITUATION

Nine at the beginning: Here you are socially unconstrained and free to act, provided you make no demands on others. It is essential that you keep your behaviour simple. You will fail if you become dissatisfied with your modest circumstances and become restless and ambitious. You must adhere to basic values.

Nine in the second place: This is the situation of a wise person who has withdrawn from the mainstream and is content to seek nothing. This person is modest and moderate, is not burdened by restlessness, and harbours no expectation or ambition.

Nine in the third place: You are very ambitious but you do not fully realise the implications of your circumstances. You are attempting something that is beyond your capabilities, and your wilfulness will lead you to disaster.

Nine in the fourth place: You are attempting a risky enterprise. You can succeed if your determination is combined with a degree of caution.

Nine in the fifth place: Your position courts danger. You can only succeed if you are totally committed to your course of action, and maintain a strict awareness of and respect for the danger at all times.

Nine at the top: If you wish to know what the future holds, just look at the fruit of your labours. All that is going to come to you is the consequence of your actions. A favourable outcome is probable if these have been good. This is the law of karma in operation.

11

PEACE

THE SCENARIO You are on the right path. This is a time when it is possible to reform all the inferior and degrading elements in your life or circumstances. This hexagram corresponds with the first month of spring, when the forces of nature are awakening. This is an ideal time for growth: a time for creating new conditions, progress and reform. Unimpeded movement is possible, as the path lies before you and suits you admirably. By realising and exploiting the potential of this time you can greatly further your aims and increase your estate.

BUSINESS IMPLICATIONS You are on the verge of a healthy and strong upward movement in the marketplace. Ideal conditions for growth, expansion, mergers, and all forms of progress exist. It is an excellent time to review work practices and to implement necessary reforms. You are on the right track: all that remains is to follow it to its logical conclusion.

LOVE IMPLICATIONS This is a very auspicious hexagram for relationships. Ideal conditions exist in which love may be instigated, fostered and furthered. Your feelings or attitudes may undergo some reform. You will experience new feelings towards, and gain a different perception of, your partner, and generally make considerable progress. This awakening process will lead to the bliss of a peaceful, compatible relationship.

SPIRITUAL IMPLICATIONS You are in harmony with

your time. The good elements of your character are in ascendancy, and it is now relatively easy to isolate and thoroughly subjugate any evil influences or tendencies of which you are aware in your character.

THE MOVING ELEMENTS IN THE SITUATION

Nine at the beginning: Now is a time to share your wealth. Be concerned for the welfare of others and allow your influence to spread widely.

Nine in the second place: There is a hidden danger here of the carelessness that can predominate in periods of small challenge, for example, peacetime. You may be surrounded by stagnation, even corruption. You must avoid cliques and factionalism. Be alert against laxity, complacency and weakness. Don't neglect potential dangers.

Nine in the third place: You must be aware that the condition of peace and prosperity must come to an end. Evil can be temporarily suspended but never totally defeated — it always returns. This is an eternal law on this plane of existence: prosperity is followed by decline. The knowledge of this can keep you from falling into illusions of security when good fortune visits. You must understand that security and good fortune arise from within the self. A change is coming. Enjoy the present with equanimity.

Six in the fourth place: Peace allows the possibility of sincere and honest communication with your peers and superiors.

Six in the fifth place: Modest impartiality and humble dealings with all people, high or low, will bring you respect and success.

Six at the top: The peaceful, favourable conditions that you have been enjoying are at an end. Inevitable changes referred to in the third place are now taking place. Resistance is useless, and recourse to force would be disastrous. All you can do is maintain your own inner peace and position within the family circle.

12

STAGNATION, STANDING STILL

THE SCENARIO This is a time of standstill, decline and stagnation. Potential has been separated from the ability to act. This time is related to autumn, when decay has set in. There is little money and no assistance at hand. Social, moral and political corruption exists. This is the hexagram of being enmeshed in the illusory material world. There will be many arbitrary and absurd misunderstandings.

When there is no wind you cannot steer your boat. Your only option at this time is to be reserved. Refuse to compromise your morals, for dishonest methods will be very tempting, and will seem to be an easy way to proceed. Patience and abstinence are essential to avoid harm. You must keep in mind that any excess on your part will attract unwelcome attention and even calamity.

BUSINESS IMPLICATIONS A depression or severe recession exists. Bribery and corruption may tempt you, as it seems necessary to business. You are advised to rationalise your operations until this period of stagnation passes.

LOVE IMPLICATIONS The relationship has become habitual and many of the positive features that were so attractive at the beginning have now disappeared, leaving you with a declining friendship and mutual distrust. Be patient and reserved, and refuse to take part in destructive or dishonest behaviour. This may be a temporary crisis, so do or say nothing now that you will regret later.

SPIRITUAL IMPLICATIONS You are standing still. Somehow you have lost your connection to your higher self. Withdraw in seclusion if possible and remain as faithful as you can to your principles. Do not be tempted by any apparently attractive offers to take part in various worldly activities. Be withdrawn and bide your time.

THE MOVING ELEMENTS IN THE SITUATION

Six at the beginning: You have no influence in this situation: you simply do not matter. Your only option is to withdraw from the prevailing political, moral and social corruption and refuse to become involved.

Six in the second place: The stagnation is common. You must endure this with patience. Accept the circumstances, but remain apart from this stagnation by adhering to your own high principles.

Six in the third place: You have allowed yourself to become corrupt. You have used morally questionable methods to obtain power or some other advantage. You know in your heart that you are unworthy and undeserving, and you feel shame, which is a positive moral event that marks the beginning of a turn for the better.

Nine in the fourth place: Here the stagnation is about to come to an end. You can act if you are genuinely motivated and feel you have a definite task to perform. Otherwise, you will fail in whatever you undertake.

Nine in the fifth place: A significant change, mostly for the better, has arrived. Yet this is a crucial period of transition when things are most likely to go wrong. Now success is only possible if you employ the greatest caution, reserve and care.

Nine at the top: This period of stagnation cannot last forever. The situation is changing, but it will take very positive efforts to turn the situation around so that there is a return to peace and prosperity. You must maintain your moral stance and get to work.

13

<u></u>

FELLOWSHIP AND FRIENDSHIP, FULFILMENT IN DIFFERENCES

THE SCENARIO This is the hexagram of community service. The ideal is to serve without selfishness. Now is a good time for communal endeavours, when success may be brought about by allying yourself with others on the basis of common purpose. Purposeful leadership would be of help. You will not be able to achieve anything alone. It is not the time of the individual.

To understand how things work would be an advantage: in order to achieve something, the elements necessary for success must be brought together. For instance, to create a fire, you need wood, air and fire itself. Without these three elements, the fire is merely potential, but when properly combined, these elements result in a fire useful for cooking, warmth and light.

To be successful in the situation represented by this hexagram, attention should be paid to the following necessary elements: a fellowship of like-minded people, some form of organisation, and firm, goal-oriented leadership. Without these elements there will be chaos and unrealised potential.

BUSINESS IMPLICATIONS Strong leadership and a highly motivated workforce is necessary at this time. Now you should develop new products or services. To get the best out of staff members, give them a sense of involvement and participation in the project. Careful planning is needed to ensure that all the elements needed for the success of the enterprise have been considered, selected, and put into place. Your project will fail if anything has been overlooked.

LOVE IMPLICATIONS Your relationship needs to fit somehow into a wider perspective, perhaps that of an extended family or some other close community. You need to be selfless, and ensure that all the ingredients of true love are present and accounted for: otherwise, this relationship will probably fail. Do not be deterred by what initially seem to be irreconcilable differences. The existence of differences between people (especially lovers) fulfils: differences are complementary and the recognition that we are fundamentally different is to be attracted.

SPIRITUAL IMPLICATIONS Unselfish, uncomplaining service to the community will be of great value to your development now.

THE MOVING ELEMENTS IN THE SITUATION

Nine at the beginning: A union among people can work now. It is most important that secret agreements do not take place, and that the union is open to all. The basic principles and aims of this union should be clearly and unambiguously presented so there is no mistake or misunderstanding.

Six in the second place: Personal, egotistic interests within a group are always a danger to the entire group. Cliques, elitism and exclusivity must be avoided since they lead to factionalism and render the group ineffectual.

Six in the third place: There is mistrust within the group: some of the members have selfish motives and interests at heart. Spying, gossip, and secret tactics are at work. This must be resolved before any progress can be made.

Nine in the fourth place: The consequences of disunity, or the failure of the union, are very great and this tends to shock opponents into possible reconciliation, which will be very beneficial to all concerned.

Nine in the fifth place: Here personal differences seem irreconcilable but the separation is superficial: in their hearts these people want the same thing. Despite severe obstacles you must cling to this union, for it is bound to eventually succeed. Openly express yourself and declare your intentions honestly: this may help overcome the superficial differences between the parties concerned.

Nine at the top: Simply joining others at this time can help, even if this union is not made with full and heartfelt conviction, but as a matter of convenience.

14

≡≡
≡≡

GREAT POSSESSION, ABUNDANCE, FULFILMENT

THE SCENARIO Here is the wealth that experience can bring: you are wise and you can foresee outcomes and consequences because of your life experience. You have a lot of energy, and you can rely on your luck to carry you through. Now drastic or extreme methods can succeed. If you are a person with some authority or power, you are advised to curb your egotism and pride, and suppress selfish motives that are not in the interest of the general good. You must not act through greed, pride, or immodesty. You are in a position to suppress what is bad in you by making obvious what is good. By using your considerable creative powers you can achieve much, and a beauty, mellow with experience, will be created.

BUSINESS IMPLICATIONS The requirements for great success are at hand. These may include partners, or simply an idea. You can adopt with confidence even the most risky plan because luck is with you at the moment.

LOVE IMPLICATIONS All misunderstanding in your relationship now vanishes. The way is clear for your love to move into a mature stage of great mutual understanding — to achieve the fulfilment for which you have always longed. A strong, mature energy arises from within and makes love work.

SPIRITUAL IMPLICATIONS You must examine yourself and your life, and bring out into the light of day what is good and bad, where it may be dispassionately examined. You must combat and curb the bad elements you find, and favour and promote the good: this is the best way to promote spiritual advancement.

THE MOVING ELEMENTS IN THE SITUATION

Nine at the beginning: You have not as yet had much opportunity to make mistakes, but this does not mean that you will not face difficulties. On the contrary, it is only by being aware that you have a lot to learn that you will be able to face and conquer ensuing problems. Avoid wastefulness, arrogance, and complacency.

Nine in the second place: You have talent and ingenuity. It is time for you to undertake something significant and important. You have assistants that you can trust.

Nine in the third place: An enlightened person realises that private property is an illusion, and that the rich are only custodians of wealth that should rightly be used to further the interests of the community. Only petty, unevolved people use their wealth for self-gratification and other selfish ends.

Nine in the fourth place: You are surrounded by people 'richer' than you. Quell your pride, do not allow yourself the corrupting luxury of envy, and don't try to compete. Be your natural self and adhere to your usual behaviour and goals.

Six in the fifth place: This signifies a situation in which honesty and accessibility are the keynotes in the relationships being formed. You are honest and open, but also dignified and serious, and nobody takes you lightly.

Nine at the top: Everything is going well, but it is important to retain your sense of balance in the face of success. You should be sensibly modest and give adequate appreciation and acknowledgement to all those who help you.

15

MODESTY, TIME TO ADAPT

THE SCENARIO This is a transitory phase, and a time for modesty. Try to make an effort to adapt yourself to the circumstances and the people around you. It is a time for balancing extremes in the situation, or in your own character, and to harmonise your interests with those of the people around you. The important thing is to be modest and unassuming, no matter how great your talents or achievements. You must understand that the affairs of humankind are like the cycles of nature. The moon, after being full, must decline; and having declined, it will again come to shine brightly in fullness. Your situation is that of the waning moon. Do not let this apparent decline bother you, for it is only a natural part of the flow governed by the law of change. You must carry things to completion, while seeking a modest balance in your life.

BUSINESS IMPLICATIONS You are at the beginning of a cyclical trade downturn. You can mitigate the effects somewhat by minimising waste in your organisation. This slightly slack period is a good time to get your house in order. Examine the workings of your business with an eye to detecting extremes in wages, duties, emphasis or dependence on a particular product or service and towards balancing these extremes. This applies especially towards your staff: extremes, in pay and responsibilities, for example, can create discontent and sow the seeds of labour dissension in the future.

LOVE IMPLICATIONS It may be that the first fiery sexual passion of the relationship is on the wane. This may be part of a cycle that revolves within your relationship: a movement in degrees of intensity. Do not worry, for it is a passing phase and a good time to assess the relationship without being blinded by passion. Now you can create more equitable and just conditions within this match.

SPIRITUAL IMPLICATIONS Seek out the extremes in your character and try to create a balance. Seek neither the high ground nor the low, but that space that is the complement of the two, the middle way. Remember that modesty and humility are important now.

THE MOVING ELEMENTS IN THE SITUATION

Six at the beginning: Difficult, dirty and dangerous jobs are best carried out as simply and quickly as possible. Avoid too much discussion or consideration of the matter in hand: just proceed. Be modest, in that you do not impose demands or hedge about matters with conditions and stipulations. Do the job that needs doing, and no complications will arise.

Six in the second place: You are a moderate person who says what you mean, and means what you say. Such behaviour will be a continuing source of success, trust and good fortune to you.

Nine in the third place: This line is a warning about fame, which is a corrupting influence that can easily dazzle you and give rise to immodest or uncharacteristic behaviour. You must remain modest, whatever your merits, and this, combined with an unwavering commitment and hard work, will be rewarded handsomely in the end.

Six in the fourth place: Balance and moderation are very important: even modesty can be carried too far. Some people use modesty as a cloak to conceal a lack of responsibility, an ineffectuality, or mediocrity. Beware of these types. Are you such a type?

Six in the fifth place: Being modest does not mean being weak. Occasionally, nothing but force is appropriate in a situation. Sometimes it is necessary to take unpleasant steps, but you should take these in a spirit of objectivity, avoiding any hint of personal offence. Also, don't brag about your strength.

Six at the top: An important part of self-discipline is taking responsibility for your own actions, and being ready to shoulder the responsibility for circumstantial problems and difficulties. When in trouble avoid the temptation of self-pity or the luxury of inaction. Real modesty sets a person to work with the principle that if you wish to change the world and make it a better place you must begin with yourself.

16

≡≡ ≡≡
≡≡ ≡≡
≡≡ ≡≡

AT REST, GATHERING ENTHUSIASM

THE SCENARIO Here you are at rest, gathering strength before you undertake some big move. This is a chance for a new beginning. However, to succeed you need to harmonise your aims and values with that of the society about you. Seek out tendencies and trends, for one of the great laws of change that governs both natural events and human life is that change always moves along the line of least resistance.

You are currently at rest, as each cycle has its period of rest. During this time you must find what constitutes the line of least resistance in your life. If you can tune into this path in the society around you, you'll be able to undertake any venture with enthusiasm, confident of success.

BUSINESS IMPLICATIONS There is a marketing opportunity available now; it is simply a matter of recognising it. Keep in mind that this opportunity is a simple and natural one: it should take almost no effort, for you need only follow a natural trend in the way that flowing water follows the course of least resistance. It is a matter of finding a product that is in harmony with society and the times.

LOVE IMPLICATIONS Your relationship can succeed brilliantly — provided you are one in your opinion of how things should proceed between you. You have a very good chance for a totally new beginning together if your values and aims are in accord.

SPIRITUAL IMPLICATIONS To maintain your enthusiasm

for the path you must adjust yourself to the particular demands of the time, remembering that your spiritual movement will take place along the line of least resistance. Try to locate this line within yourself and ensure that it is not a weakness or a bad element within yourself.

THE MOVING ELEMENTS IN THE SITUATION

Six at the beginning: You are in an inferior position: that is, you are not in command of the situation. You may well have some connections with people in authority, but do not boast about this. Any sort of egotistic arrogance will bring about bad luck.

Six in the second place: Don't be swept away by enthusiasm. Keep your feet firmly on the ground and do not be misled by any illusions. Don't flatter the people above you; nor ignore or display arrogance to those beneath you. Keep your eye out for the main chance, and when you see the very first inklings of a trend (either good or bad), take appropriate action immediately.

Six in the third place: You are losing your self-confidence and independence because of procrastination. Act NOW and save yourself.

Nine in the fourth place: Your self-confidence is an inspiration to everyone around you. It is well to exploit the co-operation that this inspires in others.

Six in the fifth place: You are under stress, which is an obstruction to your enthusiasm. Harmony in your life is not possible just now. However, the tension you are experiencing is actually positive: it keeps you on your toes and prevents you from wasting energy and time in empty activity.

Six at the top: You are deluded: you are absorbed in a false reality, perhaps in happy memories of past circumstances that no longer apply. It is time to wake up to yourself and adjust to sober reality. The outcome of such an awakening will be very favourable.

17

FOLLOWING, ADAPTATION

THE SCENARIO This is the hexagram of undemanding, un-complaining, constant service that can lead to awakening.
     You must be flexible and adaptable. Lie low and try to be of service to those around you. Don't waste any energy trying to oppose your circumstances. You are in the process of moving towards new personal form. For now, serve uncomplainingly and when the day is done, go home to enjoy comfort and rest.
     You may see yourself as a leader or innovator, and not suited to service. However, who would rule must first learn to serve. Remember, too, that no situation can be resolved unless the parties concerned adapt to it and don't exhaust themselves in futile misdirected resistance.

BUSINESS IMPLICATIONS Now the competition is too strong for you. It is not time, therefore, to devote excessive energy or resources to competition. You are advised to lie low, cultivate flexibility and adaptability, and pay close attention to developing the service aspects of your business.

LOVE IMPLICATIONS You must now devote your energy in humble, unassuming service to the ones you love. Do not waste energy in trying to shape events, or in opposing what is so patently your fate for the moment. Do your duty: you won't regret it.

SPIRITUAL IMPLICATIONS This is the hexagram of ser-vice. To further yourself on the path you must seek out unselfish service that benefits others. This will bring about changes that will lead you to the next stage of your development.

THE MOVING ELEMENTS IN THE SITUATION

Nine at the beginning: Change is occurring, and communication is necessary to find out exactly what is happening. Seek out information, not only from those who are close to you but from all sections of society, high and low, friend and foe. This is the only way to get the information you need, so that your actions will have a basis in reality.

Six in the second place: You will be judged by the company you keep: moreover, you will be shaped by this company. You must therefore choose. If you throw yourself away on bad company you will lose the people of intellectual power and good moral values who could help you.

Six in the third place: It is time to grow up. You must part company with the inferior and superficial people and elements in your life, and recognise that you must take the next step in personality development. You must decide what you want and not be led astray by passing desires and inclinations.

Nine in the fourth place: Be aware of underlings who seek personal advantage by means of flattery and attempts to be indispensable. Flatterers have their own motives: try to maintain your independence and distance from these people.

Nine in the fifth place: Everybody needs an ideal to aspire to: a lodestar. Aim high and insist on the best. Ensure that your lodestar is something good and beautiful.

Six at the top: You are about to acquire an assistant or helper whom you did not expect and whom you would prefer to reject, but you cannot. It is your destiny to work with this person.

18

≡≡
≡≡
≡ ≡

DECAY, TIME TO WORK ON
WHAT HAS BEEN SPOILED

THE SCENARIO This is a time of decay caused by a lack of maintenance. Change is most certainly needed. You are probably in a rut, and you must understand that the mere preservation of form is due only to habit, and that habit is often a pale pretence of life and an abuse of the state of freedom. The way you do things has become fixed and immovable, and is out of harmony with the changes going on around you. You must allow your fixed, rigid ways to die, so that you can proceed with new ways, in which new experiences are possible.

The decay and corruption in your life must be repaired. The first step is to recognise and isolate the corrupt elements. When making a new start care must be taken to prevent the old corruption from creeping in. Inertia and indifference must be avoided. Relapse into the old style of stagnancy is all too possible. You need decisiveness and energy. So put aside guilt, regret, despair and complacency. It is time to act.

BUSINESS IMPLICATIONS Your business is in a state of stagnation and decay. There is something wrong within: something that drastically needs not only repair and maintenance but possibly complete replacement. This may involve production methods, distribution or sales. A certain rigidity has crept into the business, a reliance on outmoded methods or products. Staff members may be too complacent and fixed in their work habits. You must phase out current operations and adopt new methods, products and possibly staff and management. This is the only way out.

LOVE IMPLICATIONS Your relationship has fallen into a state of disrepair. Guilt and neglect exist. Whatever love you once shared with your partner has been spoiled. You take each other for granted: the relationship has become habitual and your gestures towards each other are lifeless. You must immediately throw aside your indifference and apathy. Try to create a brand new phase in your relationship, or give up and leave. You owe it to both yourself and your partner not to continue this dead-end relationship that is doing neither of you any good at all. You stink of zen.

SPIRITUAL IMPLICATIONS You are in a state of rotten corruption that is an abuse of human freedom. You have fallen into a dead pretence of spirituality that is slowly killing you. You need discipline and any master would show you grandmotherly kindness by giving you a sound thrashing.

THE MOVING ELEMENTS IN THE SITUATION

Six at the beginning: You have been taught to do things in a particular way, but times have changed and the traditional way is not appropriate to your needs. Reform is necessary, which may not be easy but is essential. Be aware that danger accompanies all reform, and be ready for undesirable effects.

Nine in the second place: The current decay has been brought about by weakness, either your own or another's. Proceed slowly and sensitively to repair this decay. Drastic measures are out of order and may cause misfortune.

Nine in the third place: Anxious to rectify past mistakes you are moving too quickly. However, too much energy is better than too little in this case. You may be regarded by others as hasty or inconsiderate, but problems will be minor.

Six in the fourth place: You are in a difficult position, for you do not have the power to reverse decay and discord arising from the past. Unfortunately, the position will only get worse. You must either find strength, perhaps in the form of helpers, or quit this situation.

Six in the fifth place: Here you assume responsibility to correct an old, established corruption and institute a long-needed reform. The decay is so entrenched that a completely new beginning is not possible, but a thorough reform will greatly alleviate the situation.

Nine at the top: You may well be aware of reform needed around you, yet not everyone has an obligation to involve themselves in ordinary everyday affairs. This is the sign of the sage, who transcends the situation and aims for higher ideals, creating high values for all humanity in the future.

19

$$\equiv\!\equiv$$

SOMETHING APPROACHES

THE SCENARIO This hexagram signifies the time at the very beginning of a new cycle, and is symbolised by the period occurring immediately after the winter solstice, when the days grow longer and the rejuvenating power of spring begins to grow in influence. This is good, but there is one thing you must never forget: spring does not last forever, and in the normal course of events the signs of the time will reverse themselves and the decay of autumn will come to predominate. Therefore, you must make every effort to make full use of this joyous and creative energy while it lasts.

The time is one of positive growth, preceding inevitable, cyclical decay. The inevitable period of decay will not disturb you if you make good use of this time.

BUSINESS IMPLICATIONS A serious study of your business's past performance will reveal the existence of cycles in sales, profits and other aspects. You are right on the verge of an upturn in the cycle, which requires immediate attention if you are to obtain the maximum advantage. Be restrained in making long-term capital commitments, for instance, in production, for this upturn cannot be sustained. Upturns must be followed by downturns. Careful rationalisation of production is necessary so that the inevitable downturn does no damage.

LOVE IMPLICATIONS It's the springtime of a relationship. Understand that the first flames of hot, passionate love tend to die down and are replaced by milder feelings. This is the inevitable fate of all romantic love.

SPIRITUAL IMPLICATIONS This is a time for the spiritual person to be called upon to teach. You must be prepared to give of yourself without any limit, to be tirelessly patient and tolerant.

THE MOVING ELEMENTS IN THE SITUATION

Nine at the beginning: This is a good time for you to join other people and start something new — perhaps some communal enterprise. Don't be carried away by enthusiasm: work calmly and diligently.

Nine in the second place: You are a balanced person: you are well aware that cycles turn down as well as up. Tread your path honestly, bravely, and swiftly, and you'll enjoy a special wisdom.

Six in the third place: Everything seems to be going well for you but there is a danger that things are too easy and you might become overconfident and careless. You'll be fine if you can avoid this attitude.

Six in the fourth place: You are a person free of class, racial or sexual prejudice. This is very favourable and no problems will arise with this open-minded approach.

Six in the fifth place: You are in charge. Choose competent people to help you, then let them get on with the job. Let your experts have a free hand, and all will be done satisfactorily.

Six at the top: You show generosity and greatness. Perhaps having renounced the world, or retired, you are returning in order to teach and generally aid others. This action is good and proper now.

20

CONTEMPLATION, TAKING IN A WIDER VIEWPOINT

THE SCENARIO This is the time you should take stock: remain still for a moment and consider your life. Look at your influence on others: consider whether it is good, bad or indifferent. Take a good look at yourself. Do you like what you see? This is also an appropriate time to consider new ideas and directions.

This period of contemplation will help you realise ways that you can influence the people and situations affecting your life. If you are very wise it will be obvious to you that human affairs as well as natural events are subject to divine law. By observing the workings of these laws you can arrive at an understanding of how you can influence people and events.

Proper concentration will allow you to apprehend and understand all the mysteries of life.

BUSINESS IMPLICATIONS Take stock. Partnerships can work now. Perhaps it is time to examine the marketplace. Commission some in-depth surveys to ensure that your business is on the right tack. Examine your market penetration and the influence you hold in your field. Do you like what you see? Perhaps it's time to explore new ideas, new products, new markets and new staff.

LOVE IMPLICATIONS Take a good hard look at your relationship. If it is not all you'd like it to be, now is the opportune time to make amends. It is also a favourable time for marriage, and the resolving of misunderstandings.

If your relationship has become habitual, explore new directions in an effort to put back the zing.

SPIRITUAL IMPLICATIONS Now is the time to examine and discern how the law of the universe works and affects you personally as well as those around you. If you are pure enough, and your concentration is sufficiently profound, you apprehend the law and are at one with it. If this is the case a spiritual power will emanate from you, profoundly influencing everyone who comes into contact with you, with neither you nor they being quite aware of what is happening.

THE MOVING ELEMENTS IN THE SITUATION

Six at the beginning: You contemplate like a child: you are taking a shallow, thoughtless view of the prevailing situation. This is an inferior and unenlightened way of seeing things, as you are simply skimming the surface.

Six in the second place: You are seeing things from a limited viewpoint. Consequently, your observations and conclusions are subjective and limited. This narrow and egotistic perspective will harm you.

Six in the third place: Objective self-examination is required. You need self-knowledge (do not confuse this with idle navel-gazing). Look at the way you interact with the people and circumstances about you. In order to observe your progress, study the effects you produce.

Six in the fourth place: You must find a career or a path that suits your talents and abilities. Try to retain your independence and do not allow anyone to use you as a tool for their own purposes.

Nine in the fifth place: Examine yourself and the effect you have on others. Try to see yourself through their eyes. Assess whether you like what you see.

Nine at the top: You are a sage: liberated from both the ego and the concerns of the world. Your contemplation allows you to understand yourself and be in total harmony with the laws of life.

21

BITING THROUGH:
TAKING ACTION

THE SCENARIO An obstacle in your path can be overcome by energetic action. You are being deliberately obstructed, probably by an enemy or someone who is betraying your trust, working behind your back against you and generally blocking your progress. Compromise is impossible at this moment. Gentleness will not work: only severe measures will serve if you wish to prevent more damage.

Only reform can help now: you must actively seek out your enemy or obstacle, and act. This is a time when all your relationships should be examined with regard to their bases, aims and expectations. If you find that there are people in your life who are not measuring up, or whose behaviour is not consistent with your aims and expectations concerning them, you must act. If you find that someone has been acting against you behind your back, you must cut this person out of your life, avoiding the use of vindictive or excessive violence or revenge. Simply do what is necessary to end the relationship.

This is the hexagram of the criminal lawsuit. You must realise that unless you take vigorous action, this deliberate obstruction cannot be removed.

BUSINESS IMPLICATIONS A traitor is at work within your organisation and it may be necessary to bring criminal charges. In any case, a very vigorous investigation of all staff is required, and dismissal should follow when fault is found. Radical reform is necessary in this situation.

LOVE IMPLICATIONS There is an obstacle to the consummation of a satisfactory relationship. The problem might be within one of the partners, or it might be the result of other people meddling, perhaps telling tales. It may be you who is creating the trouble. If you do not address the situation there is no hope for the relationship.

SPIRITUAL IMPLICATIONS It may be that your aims are unclear in your mind, and you may lack a strict sense of right and wrong. If your ideas regarding spiritual discipline and law are cloudy, your path will be obscured and your activity will slacken. Reform will bring progress.

THE MOVING ELEMENTS IN THE SITUATION

Nine at the beginning: You have either just made, or are about to make, your first big mistake. Learning from this mistake will be of great advantage. If a mistake is made by another, a swift reaction in the form of just punishment will nip further trouble in the bud. It will help to realise that some people have no morals, and need to have their mistakes and transgressions corrected; otherwise they can easily graduate to more serious wrongdoing.

Six in the second place: Here it is easy to find the traitor or wrongdoer, and punishment is swift. You may be severe because of your anger, but in this case severe punishment is justified.

Six in the third place: You are in an unenviable position: you need to punish or castigate someone for doing you wrong, but you lack the authority or the power. You must try anyway. Do your best. You will earn the hatred of your enemy, but that cannot be helped.

Nine in the fourth place: Your enemies are strong, and the problem is great. Realising this you must proceed being aware that only the most continual efforts in this arduous time will lead to success.

Six in the fifth place: This is a difficult case: you are inclined to be lenient, but this will create difficulties later because you are inconsistent. You must set a standard and adhere to it.

Nine at the top: You are unable to see your own faults. You will not listen to advice, nor heed the warning that you are heading for trouble. You imagine that small 'sins' are unimportant in the scheme of things, not realising that guilt accumulates until it becomes overwhelming and can no longer be ignored.

22

GRACE, BEAUTIFUL FORM

THE SCENARIO Form rather than content is the emphasis here. It must always be kept in mind that the outer form of things may not be the essential, fundamental aspect: form, or appearance, is not what ultimately counts. Beauty does help to brighten our lives but it is not the be-all and end-all.

This hexagram symbolises a lovely time that should be enjoyed for what it is, but you must realise that this period is not likely to result in any meaningful or lasting change in your life. In fact, you should avoid making any decisions with far-reaching implications. Enjoy the beauty and harmony about you, which give an impression of order, neatness and tidiness. You should show your power by being relaxed and compliant, and avoid squandering your strength in small, unimportant matters.

BUSINESS IMPLICATIONS There isn't much happening. Perhaps it is time to attend to the cosmetic side of your operations. Get some advice on public relations, and attend to presentation and image. It is not time to attempt any significant, fundamental or far-reaching changes. Attend to the packaging, though if the product is inadequate, this will not help matters.

LOVE IMPLICATIONS Something light-hearted and perhaps quite beautiful is to be enjoyed here for what it is, but do not look for anything eternal or profound. Like froth this thing will eventually vanish. You have a superficial relationship, so don't be disappointed when you find that it has very little substance.

SPIRITUAL IMPLICATIONS Look at what you are doing. Question whether your spiritual practice is a matter of cultivating form only. Outer appearance is unimportant: ornament should be used sparingly and only in situations of no fundamental importance. You may have achieved here what seems to be perfect contemplation — desire silenced and the will at rest — but it is a temporary situation and not the way of redemption. You need to devote some serious consideration to what is fundamental and essential to your development.

THE MOVING ELEMENTS IN THE SITUATION

Nine at the beginning: You may be attracted by the chance to be pretentious and associate with your social 'betters', but you will be wiser to proceed under your own steam, simply being yourself and avoiding phoney appearances and dubious short cuts.

Six in the second place: You are in danger of being too attached to the superficial appearance of a person or a situation. You must try to ignore the superficial: look below the surface and instead attend to the inner content.

Nine in the third place: What luck! You lead a charmed life of grace and beauty. However, there is a danger that you might take things for granted and sink into a state of idleness and decadence.

Six in the fourth place: You have a choice between what seems a lovely, graceful and attractive lifestyle and a simple one. Although it may seem disappointing and difficult to renounce comforts that seem attainable, you'll find in simplicity things that can't be bought: contentment and peace of mind.

Six in the fifth place: You need to withdraw from your connections with superficial people who care only for luxury and appearance. You must strengthen your relationships with people whom you respect and admire. Remember: inner sincerity and feeling counts, not the show of material wealth.

Nine at the top: Here ornament is discarded. This is the path of simplicity: there is no need to cling to the mere form of things. The beautiful inner substance has become the form.

23

$$\begin{array}{c} \rule{3cm}{0.4pt} \ \rule{3cm}{0.4pt} \end{array}$$

SPLITTING APART, COLLAPSE, SEPARATION

THE SCENARIO The roof is about to cave in on you. This is a deteriorating position in which your efforts and intentions are being undermined by a corrupting force. You must beware of evil intentions in others. Unfortunately, there is very little you can do just now. All projects should be placed on hold until the time changes and you can remove the obstacles before you. This condition of collapse is not your fault: you should understand that in accordance with natural laws (which the *I Ching* calls 'the laws of heaven') there are constantly alternating forces at work, and it is impossible to counteract the conditions of the time.

All you can reasonably attempt to do now is stabilise your environment. When there are no tight bonds to hold things together, separation and disintegration are natural. Retreat and spin yourself a self-protecting cocoon from which you can later emerge transformed.

BUSINESS IMPLICATIONS Here are huge difficulties. Collapse is near. Some idea or venture is about to end abruptly in failure. There is no way to stave off this collapse. All you can do is consolidate. You are advised to look after your employees or others affected by the collapse, as they can help you rebuild. Stabilise the situation and keep a low profile. Remember that to rebuild, a collapse must first take place.

LOVE IMPLICATIONS Your relationship falls apart. There

is very little within this union to hold you together because you are not right for each other. When there are no true bonds between two people they separate sooner or later (usually sooner). There is nothing you can do about the situation.

SPIRITUAL IMPLICATIONS The time is not conducive to spiritual advancement. All you can do is withdraw and understand that no action whatsoever will be beneficial.

THE MOVING ELEMENTS IN THE SITUATION

Six at the beginning: Your position is being undermined by an inferior element or person. Gossip, lies, slander and innuendo are working against you. Unfortunately, there is absolutely nothing you can do but wait.

Six in the second place: Caution is the keynote here. You have no allies to aid you. Self-righteousness, or a stubborn maintenance of your untenable situation, will result in disaster. There is a probability that you may need to move quickly to save yourself when the roof caves in.

Six in the third place: You are forced into a nasty situation because of your commitments. All you can do is maintain your personal integrity, which will probably bring you into conflict with bad elements. This cannot be helped.

Six in the fourth place: Beware of danger! You are on the very edge of disaster. The collapse is imminent and can no longer be warded off. You must simply endure the inevitable and look ahead to rebuilding.

Six in the fifth place: Here is a last-minute reprieve: your potentially disastrous situation is changing for the better. Somehow moral rectitude has gained a degree of control over the unruly, corrupting forces in the situation, and collapse is averted.

Nine at the top: The collapse has happened. Better times are in sight, and rebuilding can take place. Inferior people have been totally destroyed by their self-consuming negativity. Evil destroys not only what is good; inevitably, it destroys itself.

24

THE TURNING POINT

THE SCENARIO All the energy in the universe is cyclical. This hexagram represents the low point of the cycle and is symbolised by the winter solstice, when the days begin to grow longer once more. The paths to renewal appear before you, and action gradually becomes possible. Do not be hasty: return to your old ways of doing things. Become familiar again with old friends, moods, methods and ideals, and make these things new again.

However, remember where the cycle is now. Action is unwise and precipitant. Lie low, and recognise this period as the nadir. From here there is only one way you can go — up.

BUSINESS IMPLICATIONS You have just hit rock bottom in sales and production. There is not much you can do to alleviate this, as trade, like everything else, is subject to cyclical ups and downs. However, you may take solace in the fact that downturns are inevitably followed by upturns, and from now on business will slowly but surely improve.

LOVE IMPLICATIONS You have hit a new, frosty low in your relationship. It is unwise to find fault and allocate blame. Cheer up, for the prognosis is good. If you are patient with your partner, things between you will gradually thaw, and you will soon begin to rediscover what attracted you both in the first place.

SPIRITUAL IMPLICATIONS You are at a low point. You are experiencing a sort of energy crisis. You should allow discipline to relax somewhat just now, for you can be greatly strengthened by rest. Be assured: this nadir will gradually change into a flowering.

THE MOVING ELEMENTS IN THE SITUATION

Nine at the beginning: Try not to consider an immoral idea that is against your basic principles. You must exercise some self-discipline. Adhere to what you know to be right, for even small evils have a way of taking root and growing.

Six in the second place: Seek out good company: it is much easier to do the right thing in good company. Follow good examples, and you'll be glad you did.

Six in the third place: You are restless, dissatisfied and indecisive. You imagine the grass is greener on the other side of the fence. It isn't, and if you don't learn the lesson now you will have to learn it the hard way.

Six in the fourth place: Your current surroundings and acquaintances are inferior, but there are opportunities for improvement. If you pursue chances to better yourself be aware that your path could be a lonely one. However, you could get much help from a good, strong friend.

Six in the fifth place: It is time to make a new start. You should grasp the nettle, and realise that you are responsible for your own success or failure. Face up to your faults, then make a new start. You'll never regret it.

Six at the top: You have missed the boat, which is a shame because you saw the opportunity quite clearly but you were blindly obstinate. It will be a long time before such an opportunity occurs again.

25

INNOCENCE

THE SCENARIO To be innocent you must be honestly motivated by high ideals. This time best suits a person with such motives. True success will not result from selfish or ulterior motives. Be spontaneous and try to act without hope of personal gain. This is very difficult, but if your motives are pure there is nothing to fear. Be 'innocent' — that is, unattached, for confusion does not disturb those who are detached. Perform your duties and act appropriately according to your station and circumstances.

BUSINESS IMPLICATIONS If you have been using dishonest methods, or if your business is only concerned about profits, you are headed for trouble. The role of your business should be perceived as being part of a community: if that business does not work to some degree for the good of the community as a whole, it is wrong-minded, greedy and stupid. The community is the source of profit. When it is healthy, business flourishes. When the community is poverty-stricken, business suffers as profits are diminished.

LOVE IMPLICATIONS You need to question your personal motives in this relationship. Only uncritical, unconditional love is appropriate here. If you are not purely and spontaneously in love, you are a dishonest hypocrite, and you should withdraw from the relationship, as you do not deserve this person.

SPIRITUAL IMPLICATIONS Innocence is not merely unreflecting, instinctive behaviour. It is a natural accord with the will of the cosmos. Only by devotion to the divine spirit within oneself can anybody approach the unsullied state of innocence — a state in which you act with no thought of reward or personal advantage.

THE MOVING ELEMENTS IN THE SITUATION

Nine at the beginning: Trust your own heart. Your spontaneous instincts, no matter how strange, may be followed and they will guide you to good fortune.

Six in the second place: Don't count your chickens: you should do each job that arises for its own sake without always looking forward to the results. Forget grandiose dreams of rewards and riches. Concentrate on the job in hand.

Six in the third place: You are suffering an undeserved misfortune, perhaps a robbery. It's a shame, but there is nothing to be done. The ownership of property carries with it the danger that it can be stolen. Don't lose your faith in human nature, however.

Nine in the fourth place: Resist the influence of others and know this truth: you cannot lose what really belongs to you, even when you try to throw it away. (Likewise, you cannot possess what is not really yours.) Do not worry.

Nine in the fifth place: An unexpected evil or stroke of bad luck occurs. This is not your fault. There is nothing to do but allow the situation to run its course. The matter will fix itself.

Nine at the top: The time is not ripe for action. Do nothing for the moment. Do not attempt anything new, nor try to push ahead, because you will fail.

26

GREAT POWER

THE SCENARIO This is a situation of immense potential. Very powerful energies are latent within you or your situation. It is time to undertake large and ambitious projects. Good contacts can be made now. Also, you have potential healing power, so that you can ease the sick, pacify the quarrelsome and resolve long-standing problems.

This energy depends entirely on your resolution and strength: you need to reaffirm it daily to maintain its effectiveness. Your regular habits and behaviour are not appropriate at this time, when there are tremendous amounts of energy available for use.

This is a time to try out daring new projects. There is so much energy present that it is impossible for you to lead a quiet life.

BUSINESS IMPLICATIONS A great amount of highly creative energy that should be put to use is latent within you or your organisation. All new projects, especially large-scale, high-risk, high-capital undertakings, may be commenced with every confidence. If there is no apparent energy available, you should focus on staff and production facilities for hidden potential.

LOVE IMPLICATIONS This is a relationship that can work. There is potential in this partnership for great energy that can transform you both and bring the possibility of total success in whatever you attempt.

SPIRITUAL IMPLICATIONS There is a hint here of hidden treasure, which is traditional wisdom contained in the works and words of the wise. Be familiar with, and nourish yourself with, this wisdom. Adhere to all the traditional spiritual values which you should put into practice. You might choose to help others, thus giving current validity to the old teachings. Meditation in action is far superior to meditation in isolation and repose.

THE MOVING ELEMENTS IN THE SITUATION

Nine at the beginning: You feel a strong impulse to proceed with energy. Unfortunately, there are insurmountable obstacles at this time. You must wait for the opportunity that is just around the corner. Now is not the time to act.

Nine in the second place: Your current project has failed and there is absolutely nothing you can do. Success is impossible. Bide your time and allow your energy and strength to accumulate for the big project that will appear later.

Nine in the third place: An obstacle has been removed and it is possible to proceed with a major project. A strong character with good ideas might be in the picture. A definite goal would help you shape and control your energy.

Six in the fourth place: In the past, problems have made you strong. You can easily control and use the vigorous, even wild, energy of this time.

Six in the fifth place: You are faced with a difficulty, perhaps a very strong enemy who is too strong to be attacked head-on. Find a less direct solution.

Nine at the top: All obstacles in your path have been removed. Your stored energy can now be put to use, and a notable success is possible.

27

NOURISHMENT, NURTURING SUPPORT

THE SCENARIO We need nourishment to survive physically, mentally and spiritually. Proper nourishment is important. Attention should be paid to diet, but an examination of mental and spiritual nourishment is crucial, too. Now reappraisal is necessary. Look closely at what you are doing: is it really what you want to be doing? Question whether you are living the kind of fulfilling and purposeful life that you would like, or whether you are labouring away at tasks that serve no purpose other than making a living. If you are dissatisfied, now is the time to decide what you would really like to do, then do it.

Ensure that you only allow nourishing and harmonious elements to have any effect on you. You would not choose to eat rotten meat or vegetables: likewise, corrupt spiritual and mental influences should be avoided. Be careful of what you absorb.

Consider whether you have a nourishing effect on the people you care about. Avoid negative thoughts and situations, and realise that through nurturing and support, all sorts of aims — social, personal and political — can be achieved.

BUSINESS IMPLICATIONS There are two main implications here. One concerns your support for your staff. People are more productive when they are properly nourished, that is, when they are adequately looked after by their employer. Benevolence is wise, because it increases productivity. Better wages and conditions will pay for themselves.

The second implication regards the business itself. Ask yourself whether it is getting the nourishment necessary to ensure success. The right ingredients in the diet would include, among other things, the right people for the job, adequate raw materials, a ready market, and adequate transport. A business can only flourish when all the necessary ingredients for a healthy enterprise are present.

LOVE IMPLICATIONS Love needs nourishment. It grows fat and happy on small things, like consideration, gentleness and honesty. Take a close look at your relationship. Is it nice and plump, full of health and energy? Or is it thin and pitiful, in need of nurturing support? If you wish to maintain your relationships, you must be certain that they are all adequately maintained, with the due attentions that love deserves and demands.

SPIRITUAL IMPLICATIONS Your body, mind and spirit have what could be termed 'inferior' and 'superior' parts. You must never injure or compromise superior parts for the sake of any temporary advantage of the inferior parts. If you cultivate the inferior parts of your spiritual self, you are an inferior person. You must concentrate on the higher parts of the self. Therefore, cultivate only that which nourishes and is harmonious with your higher, superior nature.

THE MOVING ELEMENTS IN THE SITUATION

Nine at the beginning: You are a person fit to be free, independent and self-reliant. However, base inferior elements within your character, like discontent and envy, can spoil this. Petty jealousies cause you to lose your dreams and misfortune will result.

Six in the second place: You are in the position of using improper methods or inappropriate people to fill your needs: you are the sort of person who is very selfish and dedicated to the pursuit of your own advantage, which will lead to trouble.

Six in the third place: You are indulging in greed, but your craving for superficial gratification does not really nourish you. You are looking in all the wrong places, and your selfish, sensual behaviour will result in no positive benefits at all.

Six in the fourth place: You are here in a position where you can help or nourish others. However, you need help from other people in order to achieve this. Keep an eye out for the right assistance.

Six in the fifth place: There is a big job to be done but you lack the strength to do it alone. Therefore, you must go against your normal methods and seek out help from a reliable person. If you proceed alone you will certainly fail. You must be aware that you are, at this moment, dependent.

Nine at the top: You are a person of great ability and, consequently, you bear a heavy responsibility to other people. If you keep this in mind, you can undertake even very complex and difficult tasks.

28

RIGIDITY, STRESS, STRAIN

THE SCENARIO This is a dangerous time because matters are strained to breaking point. Careful planning is required to avoid being caught up in the general collapse.

At this time, unsupported elements will certainly collapse, and inflexible elements will break. This process of collapse has a positive side, as it is a period of transition that provides opportunities. Firstly, you must understand that before something can be rebuilt, it must be knocked down; to be reborn you must first die. In the process of falling, support will be found. You should, therefore, take a fearless, positive stance and remain undaunted no matter what you have to give up in this seemingly disastrous time.

BUSINESS IMPLICATIONS There is disaster, a total collapse. The roof is caving in. There is nothing you can do, and little to be salvaged from the wreckage. The best course may be to walk away and begin again elsewhere. At the very least, a total rebuilding will be necessary before there is a return to normal conditions. Try to see this collapse as the beginning of new possibilities and opportunities, and treat the present as a period of transition.

LOVE IMPLICATIONS This relationship is breaking apart. There has always been something wrong here. Perhaps one of you is too rigid in your approach or attitude to sharing. Perhaps there was never quite enough feeling to sustain the partnership. In any case, the separation will turn out for the best, for it will give both of you an opportunity to meet other people and perhaps find true love, or at least a more satisfactory relationship.

SPIRITUAL IMPLICATIONS There is a basic weakness at the centre of your spiritual practices. A major reorganisation is necessary now. It may be that it is time for you to completely renounce the world and withdraw. If so, do it fearlessly and without regret, and be confident that you are entering a higher path.

THE MOVING ELEMENTS IN THE SITUATION

Six at the beginning: When you begin an enterprise, it pays to take great care when you lay the foundations. Pay attention to all the details at the very beginning (even be overcautious), for you'll be rewarded later.

Nine in the second place: Your situation is unusual, and it is necessary for you to find appropriate assistance. Finding this assistance may mean an odd matching, like an old man marrying a young girl, but it will lead to a period of extraordinary regrowth.

Nine in the third place: Accepting no advice, you just blunder ahead. Those around you will withdraw their support, and collapse will be inevitable.

Nine in the fourth place: Careful planning and someone's help successfully stave off disastrous collapse. Try to avoid selfish motives: act for the general good.

Nine in the fifth place: The status quo is maintained and collapse avoided, but this only promotes a barren stasis, wherein no renewal can occur.

Six at the top: Here is the line of sacrifice. A climax is being reached. You bravely try to accomplish your purpose, which leads you into danger. Great sacrifice to obtain your ends may be necessary. There are some things more important than life or mere continuance of the status quo.

29

AN ABYSS, DEEP WATER

THE SCENARIO Unfortunately, this is a time of general bad luck in most aspects of your life. Actual danger and real loss can occur. You may be confronted with unfamiliar situations. Everything is subject to a general downward trend. The only way to manage the demands of the time is not to resist change. You may be tempted to find support in old habits, which could be dangerous, for these old supports may be in the process of vanishing. If you find no support, you must move on. The only way to escape danger is to go right ahead. If you hesitate, you allow danger to approach. The image in the *I Ching* is that of water rushing through a steep defile, and implies that a person can escape the danger of this time by simply rushing through it. Despite the apparent downward trend of things, you will be carried out of danger if you roll with the flow. Do not allow the danger or difficulty of the time to force a compromise of your ethics.

BUSINESS IMPLICATIONS Adhere to approved policy. There are problems and there is nothing for it but to let this general downturn run its course. Things will bottom out sooner or later. When this happens preventative measures against a repetition of this downturn may be taken.

LOVE IMPLICATIONS The relationship seems to have taken a turn for the worse. It is a time of testing and challenge. There are two possibilities here. Either you abandon this relationship or you assess whether your love is true or merely a fair-weather phenomenon. If your love is true your relationship will survive, whole and uninjured, the twists and turns of this trial.

SPIRITUAL IMPLICATIONS Goodness, concentration, and other desirable and necessary spiritual attributes should not be of accidental or isolated occurrence: they should be an established part of your character. You must be consistent. It is only through repetition and practice that you will make the material that you wish to master your own.

THE MOVING ELEMENTS IN THE SITUATION

Six at the beginning: You have allowed danger and evil to become commonplace in your life. You have lost your way, and ill-fortune naturally results. A whole new start in another place at another time is necessary.

Nine in the second place: You are in a very dangerous situation. Don't be like a drowning person who thrashes wildly about. Concentrate on keeping your head above water.

Six in the third place: You are in danger that you do not fully understand. It is imperative that you stay still, which may be difficult and unpleasant, but any action you take now will only worsen the trouble and the danger. Wait until a very obvious and clear way out comes to light.

Six in the fourth place: In times of danger there is no point in standing on ceremony. A simple, honest and direct approach is required. An offer of mutual help and assistance in this crisis will help.

Nine in the fifth place: You are very ambitious, which will cause you quite a few problems. You are trying to achieve too much, when all you need do is get out of danger. You should follow the line of least resistance, but this apparently goes against your grain.

Six at the top: This is a total disaster. Nothing will work now. You are too entangled in your problems, and the way out is blocked. You have no choice but to live through the consequences of your mistakes.

30

≡ ≡
≡ ≡
≡ ≡

FIRE AND BRIGHTNESS, DEPENDING ON OTHERS

THE SCENARIO Freedom is not the normal state of the ordinary human being. It can be said that humans live in a state of conditioning, with many limitations. One way of minimising this state of bondage is to recognise and enthusiastically embrace the obligations (like the necessity of earning a living) that our conditioned state compels us to undertake. It will help if you do not fight against, but simply submit to your fate. Try to work with other people whose aims are similar to yours, and you will achieve much.

You are dependent. Only willing co-operation with others will permit you to succeed.

BUSINESS IMPLICATIONS A merger is indicated here. It is apparent that your individual success at this time depends very much upon the co-operation of others. You must avoid conflict and contention, and take second place if necessary.

LOVE IMPLICATIONS You are in love and deeply dependent on your partner. You must recognise this dependence and allow it to be a major portion of your consciousness: without your partner you are nothing. Stop trying to establish dominance or independence, as you have neither. All you can do is submit gracefully to the flaming beauty and erotic power of your partner.

SPIRITUAL IMPLICATIONS You need now to cultivate docility, like that of the calm and highly productive domestic cow. You must cultivate an attitude of compliance and voluntary dependence on the people and forces that surround you. You are conditioned and unfree, which is the natural state of human beings. See to it that you are conditioned and controlled by the mighty, harmonious, and beneficial energy that creates and drives the cosmos, and not by lesser powers and forces.

THE MOVING ELEMENTS IN THE SITUATION

Nine at the beginning: Your life at present is full of haste and activity. It is easy to allow life to sweep you along. You feel bombarded by impressions and advice. Try to be calm and concentrate on the job in hand, especially if you are just starting on some project, for the beginning contains the basis of all that will follow, and small errors now will become great problems later.

Six in the second place: Be reasonable and moderate in your dealings and your desires. Indulge yourself in no excesses. Good fortune lies in the middle way.

Nine in the third place: Life is short. Some people are tempted to enjoy it in any way they can, while others tend to be pessimistic and yield to a sense of futility and melancholy. Both attitudes are incorrect. The way lies in acceptance. You may die young or old; it doesn't matter. Accept your lot in life, and cultivate yourself spiritually and intellectually. It is your task to find out who you are. Get on with it.

Nine in the fourth place: You are excitable and restless. You are full of nervous energy, which only serves to exhaust you. You spend your power too quickly, like a meteor that flashes briefly across the sky and is gone.

Six in the fifth place: You are at a climax of sorts. It is time to put aside all hopes for the future and regrets of the past. You need a change of heart. Try to understand the vanity of all conventional human striving, and resist the temptation to indulge in grief for the past. Wisdom could be yours now.

Six at the top: Be kind to yourself, for everyone has some bad habits. You should root out those that are genuinely harmful, and tolerate those that are merely eccentric and harmless. Too much of anything, including self-discipline and self-approbation, is worse than too little.

31

$$\begin{array}{c}\text{▬▬▬ ▬▬▬}\\\text{▭▭▭ ▭▭▭}\\\text{▭▭▭ ▭▭▭}\\\text{▬▬▬ ▬▬▬}\end{array}$$

COURTSHIP, WOOING, BEING ATTRACTED

THE SCENARIO This is a very cheerful and attractive hexagram, which often represents courtship and marriage. Choosing to marry now will bring you good fortune (though you must never forget that good luck requires courage). This is successful mating — a joyful discovery of how elements can fit together in harmony. It is important that the man, or yang principle, places himself in a position of deference, below the woman, or yin principle, showing consideration for the 'weaker' sex.

The implications of this situation are many: you should allow yourself to be acted upon and influenced by the person (or project or object) that you seem to find so interesting. You must be prepared to allow yourself to be affected and changed. The correct attitudes to adopt are those of openness, and acceptance and toleration of others. Welcome those who approach. The key concept here is courtship, rather than seduction.

BUSINESS IMPLICATIONS A merger is strongly implied here, a friendly marriage that will greatly advantage both parties involved by increasing business and offering excellent prospects for the future.

LOVE IMPLICATIONS A serious courtship, with the honourable, traditional intentions of formal marriage, is indicated here. There is love, romance and attraction, and it is time to grasp the hand offered you, and to fulfil yourself in a union that gives you what you lack and makes up for anything you have missed. To marry is the best thing you could do.

SPIRITUAL IMPLICATIONS Your mind must be kept humble and free. You must be open to formative influences and good advice. When people think they know it all, others soon cease offering advice and assistance. Guard against having a closed mind.

THE MOVING ELEMENTS IN THE SITUATION

Six at the beginning: There seems to be some movement or potential attraction in the air. Don't rely too heavily on this: it is of little significance.

Six in the second place: Something seems to be happening, but it may be something wrong that will only lead you astray. You should avoid acting on the issue until you are completely certain of its nature.

Nine in the third place: You are experiencing a strong impulse of the heart to act decisively but, if you proceed, you will certainly regret it. You may have decided not to kowtow to a person of influence or not to yield to every whim of your lover. It is dangerous to indulge without restraint your own whims, for the basis of human freedom is self-control.

Nine in the fourth place: Acting on the dictates of the heart is fine, providing you have a good and constant heart. Do not be calculating or manipulative in this situation; otherwise, you will only exhaust yourself and no good will come of it.

Nine in the fifth place: Shallow people achieve nothing. If you are a closed personality, impervious to outside influence, the world will be equally uninfluenced by you. You'll achieve nothing.

Six at the top: You are full of ideas and words. Be aware that words are only words — sounds that come from our mouths. To have value, ideas must be put into action. Mere words are insignificant and no substitute for action.

32

LASTING DEVELOPMENT, DURATION

THE SCENARIO This is the hexagram of continuation. You should rely on methods and policies that have been useful in the past. You may now be able to see how ceremony, custom and tradition are useful, serving a purpose in the here and now.

This situation also stands for ripeness and maturity, which should not be allowed to deteriorate into stagnation. Maturity, as in middle age, is not invariably a signal of decline. It is a normal part of natural change. There is more than one stage in life. We pass through many stages and life doesn't end until we die. By continually renewing life and embracing change as it occurs we may obtain lasting development and duration. Do not allow yourself to be left behind. Keep abreast of your changes, and encourage new conditions to grow naturally out of the old.

BUSINESS IMPLICATIONS Your business or product has reached a point of saturation or maturity, and it may appear that the only way to go from here is down. However, instead of sinking into decline and decay, you could fight this tendency with careful modifications of your operations or your products and/or services. Look at the history of your business, as you may find there an important indication of the path that can lead to a prosperous future.

LOVE IMPLICATIONS You are in a dynamic relationship that, like everything else in this material dimension, is subject to change. You have reached one plateau of maturity.

You may not feel as passionate as you did when you first got together as a couple, but this does not mean that you are no longer in love. The nature of love is such that it matures into something greater than mere physical coupling. Your relationship is not in decline: it is going through a necessary and natural change, a kind of renewal with a shift in the emphasis. Enjoy this stage of your love.

SPIRITUAL IMPLICATIONS Your spirituality is not dependent on rigidity and immobility of character and thought. As you progress on the spiritual path, you will find that your outlook must change as you and your circumstances do. You understand more every day. The only thing that should remain fixed is your basic inner aim: enlightenment.

THE MOVING ELEMENTS IN THE SITUATION

Six at the beginning: You are being too hasty by trying to change too much too quickly. You can't change the situation overnight, as you'll soon discover. Move slowly and accomplish changes gradually, or you shall achieve nothing.

Nine in the second place: This is a time to avoid extremes. You may feel underemployed; that there is no real challenge to your abilities. Avoid the temptation to search for something else to do. Apply yourself to what you are doing right now. Tread water and avoid extremes.

Nine in the third place: You are inconsistent and too easily affected by happenings around you. As long as you remain at the mercy of your changing moods you will have unhappy experiences. You must cultivate a consistent self that is not at the mercy of outside influence and happenstance.

Nine in the fourth place: Your goals are unrealistic. You are looking for things in all the wrong places. No matter how persistent or diligent you are, you will fail.

Six in the fifth place: Following traditional ways and using conservative techniques may not always suit the job in hand. You need to learn how to apply effective methods to each job that arises. You will have to learn how to innovate, and deviate from accepted methodology when it is necessary.

Six at the top: You are too anxious. You are a driven person who has never learned to relax. You have no inner composure. This prevents real efficiency and will invite misfortune.

33

RETREAT, STRATEGIC WITHDRAWAL

THE SCENARIO The forces of decay and dissolution are on the rise. Avoid confrontation, because you cannot fight what is happening head-on. Only retreat is safe. Fate is against you at the moment. You should avoid travel, watch what you say, and do not instigate lawsuits. Keep out of the way of people who can do you harm, and remain calm. Do not waste your energy on anger or hatred, for it is (or should be) beneath you to indulge in such base emotions. Remember that hatred binds us to the hated object or person in the same way that love binds.

Retreat is not dishonourable. It is a strategic withdrawal. You don't surrender you withdraw slowly, making it difficult for any enemy to advance without exposing themselves to a desperate struggle.

BUSINESS IMPLICATIONS Now is a worrying time, as fate is against you. You are advised not to get involved in any co-operative ventures or mergers. It may be that a merger in which you are already involved is going sour. Don't try to tackle the matter head-on, and, above all, don't institute legal proceedings, as you'll lose. All you can do is duck for cover. Begin your retreat, avoid direct conflict, and try to consolidate for a better time later. All situations are temporary.

LOVE IMPLICATIONS The relationship has gone sour. A dark element is affecting you as a couple. This element might be jealousy, selfishness, or any negative emotion, and is taking over. Unfortunately, the indication is that there is very little you can do to rescue this relationship. The forces of decay are on the rise. The best thing to do is withdraw from the relationship as gracefully as you are able.

SPIRITUAL IMPLICATIONS You must neutralise your feelings towards people who happen to influence your life negatively. You must never allow hatred to enter your mind or heart, for hatred, like love, is a form of subjective involvement that binds you to the object or person you hate. You must learn how to quietly retreat into the inner realms of thought, where hatred cannot reach.

THE MOVING ELEMENTS IN THE SITUATION

Six at the beginning: You are hard-pressed by an enemy or a destructive force that is almost upon you. You should have withdrawn long before this stage. It is now too late to retreat. You are advised to do nothing.

Six in the second place: You are in trouble and need to retreat. You need help, and you will probably take it, willingly or otherwise, from any source that offers.

Nine in the third place: You are trying to retreat, but have been held back. Now you are in difficulties. You may be forced to use questionable methods or people to make good your escape. This is a difficult choice. You may escape but little will be accomplished.

Nine in the fourth place: It is time to retreat, avoiding violence or emotional turmoil. If you are in the right, this retreat will bring you luck; if not, you face degeneration.

Nine in the fifth place: It is time to retreat. If you are wise you will leave willingly and graciously in a friendly manner. Do not allow yourself to be delayed or dissuaded. Just go.

Nine at the top: Retreat now, without guilt or doubt. You are free, the way ahead is clear, and you may go in all confidence. You are doing the right thing, and good fortune will result.

34

$$\begin{array}{cc} \rule{1.5em}{0.08em}\quad\rule{1.5em}{0.08em} \\ \rule{1.5em}{0.08em}\quad\rule{1.5em}{0.08em} \\ \rule{4em}{0.08em} \\ \rule{4em}{0.08em} \\ \rule{4em}{0.08em} \end{array}$$

THE POWER OF THE STRONG

THE SCENARIO You are in a position of strength and power. It seems as though you are able to do anything you want but, in fact, you are being tested for strength of character and morals. Use your authority and power to improve your relationships, and do good works if you possibly can. It will be to your advantage to behave in a strictly orthodox manner. Adhere strictly to established convention.

The biggest danger that faces a powerful person is the temptation to act wilfully without regard for morality. A further problem is that your strength may make you impatient and impetuous: the consequence of this is that you do not wait for the right time to act, and your strength becomes brute force.

It is necessary to develop the qualities of mercy and compassion in order to handle power properly.

BUSINESS IMPLICATIONS Business is booming and you are a power in the marketplace, or in your particular field. You must use this economic muscle to help improve conditions in your community, and to improve your product. Do not use your power to grind any opposition into bankruptcy. Strength, and justice — social, economic, and personal — must be united.

LOVE IMPLICATIONS You have a great deal of influence and power over another person. You owe it to yourself and your partner to exercise this power with compassion, love and mercy. If you are tempted to abuse your strengths, you will regret it. Your partner is totally in love with you, and depends on you for virtually everything. You are the source of all happiness and all misery for this person. Your behaviour should be positive, affirming, loving, encouraging and caring.

SPIRITUAL IMPLICATIONS You have power, and it is most important that all your actions are in strict accord with what is correct. If you have any doubts about the morality of any of your planned endeavours, you should think again. Your power is such that you could do great harm if your actions are not moral.

THE MOVING ELEMENTS IN THE SITUATION

Nine at the beginning: You are strong, but you are in the wrong place. If you try to force an issue you will be making a mistake, for in this case you lack the authority to enforce your wishes.

Nine in the second place: Things are going your way at last. However, you must be on your guard against overconfidence, which is the only thing that can spoil the situation for you.

Nine in the third place: You are strong, but you must conceal your power. To display and boast about your strength is tempting, but if you do this, you'll find yourself entangled in all sorts of problems. Do not revel in your power. Do not flaunt it in empty display.

Nine in the fourth place: You must use your power sparingly and gradually wear down resistance and problems, rather than using brute force, to crash your way through. Your strength is not wasted on external display: it is concentrated on getting the job done.

Six in the fifth place: You have won. The situation has eased and you no longer have anything to prove. Don't be stubborn. Let go and relax.

Six at the top: You have gone too far in your use of force and now find yourself in a deadlock. Your efforts only serve to complicate matters further. You must drop your obstinacy. Everything will be fine if you stop trying to force matters.

35

☰☰

PROGRESS: NATURAL, POSITIVE CHANGE

THE SCENARIO You are on the move, which is good. You will encounter new people and forge new relationships that will help you to grow as a person. Take your time when making decisions. Wait until a good omen appears, or until you have a definite feeling that the time is right: then act. There are excellent prospects for clear communication and mutual accord. Having decided to act, you must put yourself forward and show your talents, abilities and intelligence.

This hexagram is symbolised by the rising sun: light spreads, diminishing darkness and obscurity, and allowing much positive, progressive activity.

BUSINESS IMPLICATIONS Extraordinarily good luck in business is possible if you make the right decision. This is a time of natural and positive change. You must look ahead in planning. New relationships, like mergers, and new products and services, are possible now. Be bold in implementing new ideas, for they will lead to growth.

LOVE IMPLICATIONS There is a fine possibility for mutual accord. This is like a new day dawning in your relationship. Will it be like all the other days you have shared? Or will it be something new? Show your love, compassion and intelligence to each other. Are not such attributes admirable and lovable? Now you can accomplish much growth in your relationship. It is natural and proper that you should grow as a couple. The alternative to growth is stagnation and separation.

SPIRITUAL IMPLICATIONS The pure spiritual nature of humankind is like a mirror or a window that has become clouded or obscured by constant contact with material things here on the physical plane. Before your light can shine forth you must cleanse your window of the dross and shadow of illusion.

THE MOVING ELEMENTS IN THE SITUATION

Six at the beginning: Other people seem to lack confidence in you. Do not be angry about this. Let generosity and charm smooth things over for you. Just attend to the work in hand, and things will turn out all right.

Six in the second place: Your progress is halted because of a lack of communication with a superior. You can only do your best. Persevere with your duty and the situation will resolve itself.

Six in the third place: You are working with others, which is good. A common trust exists. You may depend on these people to help you over difficult patches, just as they can depend on you. This trust leads to good fortune.

Nine in the fourth place: You have chosen a questionable way to profit in this situation. Remember that your conduct is dangerous, for the truth about your activities is bound to come out into the open.

Six in the fifth place: You are in an influential position. You could easily abuse your position for personal profit, but it would not be moral to do so. You benefit yourself and others far more by being non-mercenary.

Nine at the top: You may be aggressive, severe and offensive with yourself, but if you try these tactics on other people you will alienate them and create many problems.

36

DARKNESS ENCROACHES, LIGHT FADES

THE SCENARIO This is a time of censorship, difficulty and danger. Your enemy is gaining power and influence. You must step into the background and conceal your real feelings and ideals. Avoid quarrels and confrontation, for you have no power. There is a 'malignant star' shining on you. Do not, however, allow yourself to be swept along by unfortunate circumstances and bad luck. The trick is to roll with the flow and adapt. Be flexible, yielding, tractable. This may entail your surrendering your aims and ambitions for the moment. Hide your light under a bushel, lie low and be non-judgemental, but don't let your standards slip.

BUSINESS IMPLICATIONS Bad news. You can do nothing: the market is down, and there is possibly an inferior product or service undercutting your business. Perhaps a competitor is using unfair or illegal practices to rob you of trade. Your only option is to adapt to the demands of the time. If possible, avoid compromising your sense of right and wrong.

LOVE IMPLICATIONS There is something nasty happening to your relationship. Some dark element, like selfishness, greed, or jealousy, is predominating. The life-enhancing and light-giving elements like sharing and unconditional acceptance are in retreat. There is nothing you can do, except adapt to the changing circumstances and try not to compromise your morals.

SPIRITUAL IMPLICATIONS It is time to lie low. If you try to rise, or display your spiritual nature, you'll attract hostility. Be careful to maintain your high standards. Do not be influenced by the practices and standards of others, but do not criticise the practices of others, nor try to throw light into dark corners of other people's behaviour. In this time of darkness, do not try to show how illuminated or knowing you are. Without allowing yourself to be fooled, let things that are not quite right pass by without comment or censure.

THE MOVING ELEMENTS IN THE SITUATION

Nine at the beginning: The situation is difficult: you might try to rise above the situation, but this will attract a hostile reaction. You can retreat, and evade the issue. If you are determined not to compromise your principles, you will be forced to suffer some deprivation. If you persist with personal aims, it is also certain that you'll be misunderstood, and you'll be spoken against.

Six in the second place: You have suffered a setback. The odds are against you, yet you persist in acting in the interests of other people, which will benefit you in the long run. The setback may contain a valuable lesson.

Nine in the third place: By sheer chance you have an opportunity to nip the trouble in the bud. Don't try to rush matters, however, as there are deep-seated difficulties. Move slowly, with care.

Six in the fourth place: You have a good understanding of the nature of the trouble surrounding you. You, therefore, understand there is absolutely nothing you can do, except leave the scene before the inevitable disaster occurs.

Six in the fifth place: You are trapped and simple escape is not an option. There is nothing to do but retreat into your own spirit. You can't fight the evil, but it is possible, by exercising much caution, to protect yourself.

Six at the top: The situation is as bad as it can get, and now it can only improve. Be patient and wait for the better time now dawning.

37

THE FAMILY, NOURISHING RELATIONSHIPS

THE SCENARIO This is the time to seek and find your natural and comfortable role in the scheme of things. You must cultivate fidelity and loyalty, thereby giving substance to your role. Opposites may now mature in harmony. If you are female, you should understand the great power of the woman, and that you are the very pillar of the family. The family is society in miniature, and the tie that holds the family together is the intelligence, patience, unselfishness and loyalty of the woman. If you are male, you should understand that you must provide the woman with strength and support, and behave with the appropriate loving reverence.

Say what you mean, and mean what you say. Be consequent in your behaviour. Teach by example, for your credibility depends on your words being supported by your behaviour. If you do not act with loving respect your situation will disintegrate.

BUSINESS IMPLICATIONS Establish firm roles within your business. Make the lines of demarcation clear, so all staff members know what their job is within a well-defined system. In this way your business will function smoothly and easily. There may be a merger in the wind that could greatly benefit you, as long as you are certain what role your business must take in the relationship. Decisions need to be made as to whether it is a supportive or an actively innovative role, and whether or not that role suits your outlook and capabilities.

LOVE IMPLICATIONS This is the hexagram of the family. The implication is that you are ripe for marriage or commitment. If you are single, you should start thinking about the future. If you are married or with a partner, you must give thought and substance to your role. To have a good husband or wife or partner, you must be a good husband or wife or partner. Cultivate natural love and affection.

SPIRITUAL IMPLICATIONS Establish firm spiritual practices from the beginning. Bad habits, like self-indulgence, laziness, and giving in to passing whims and passions, are very easily established, and once established are very difficult to eradicate. Therefore, accustom yourself to obeying an established set of rules that will help to protect you from the negative effects of bad habits.

THE MOVING ELEMENTS IN THE SITUATION

Nine at the beginning: Establish firm roles. A family, or any other social unit, needs well-defined roles so all members know their place. Try to impose order so that discipline is present. Anarchy, with everybody indulging their own whims and passions, is detrimental to the family or social unit.

Six in the second place: You are currently doing an important job. Do not allow yourself to be distracted or to become restless. Do not try to force events or situations; otherwise, there will be trouble. Adhere to your task, be it mothering or fathering. Good things are in store.

Nine in the third place: There is trouble within the family. Tempers are flaring. Moderation and forbearance can help here. Allow people to be individuals within the confines of the family. Only be severe if the situation is chaotic and threatens to disintegrate the family.

Six in the fourth place: This is the line of the faithful, ideal wife, who is a sound economic manager. Be modest and humble, and good luck will result.

Nine in the fifth place: This is the line of the ideal husband, who is magnanimous, loving and gentle. He is not a figure that inspires fear. The whole family trusts him, because love governs his transactions with his wife and children.

Nine at the top: Whether or not this family holds together depends entirely on you. If your character fits the role you are in, your natural sense of responsibility will bring good fortune.

38

$$\overline{\underline{\quad\quad}}\ \overline{\underline{\quad\quad}}$$

OPPOSITION AND CONTRADICTION

THE SCENARIO This is a time of estrangement, contradiction and opposition. You find misunderstanding and difficulty in everything. Major projects are completely out of the question, but it may be possible to proceed with minor projects, because the opposition you face does not preclude all agreement. Some opposition can be constructive: as when it forms a polarity, creating the tension of opposites, as in man and woman, light and dark. When opposites are reconciled and in balance, they lead to creation and reproduction. But if the opposition you face is not of the magical, polarising type, withdrawal is advised. Just stick to small matters.

BUSINESS IMPLICATIONS You are frankly losing ground to competitors in the marketplace, and you may be affected by an internal power struggle and a clash of ambitions. There is no chance of achieving any major successes. Forget any big projects you have on the drawing board. You can succeed only in small, inconsequential matters now.

LOVE IMPLICATIONS You and your partner are at odds. Although you both have the same goals, you have different ways of doing things. This discord makes life unnecessarily hard for you both. Perhaps you could tap into the dynamic tension that your man-woman energies create. Otherwise, you could separate now, your relationship degenerating into quarrels and angry opposition. Such a pity, considering you both, in fact, want the same thing.

SPIRITUAL IMPLICATIONS If you are a spiritual person, it is vital that you always avoid baseness, meanness or vulgarity. You may have to mix within a community (most people do), but you should never allow spiritually infererior persons to affect you. Avoid being negatively influenced, and retain your individuality.

THE MOVING ELEMENTS IN THE SITUATION

Nine at the beginning: There is opposition and estrangement. If you try to force the issue, you'll make matters worse. Wait patiently until matters resolve themselves, for things will work out naturally.

Nine in the second place: Misunderstandings prevent you from meeting and working with people necessary for your success right now. However, an unexpected encounter will be very lucky for you.

Six in the third place: You are experiencing many difficulties. It seems that luck is against you. You have begun badly and people have insulted you. Despite this, if you can stick to the job there is a good chance that things will resolve themselves.

Nine in the fourth place: You are in an isolated position, because you are not in agreement with those around you. There is a possibility of acquiring a friend, whom you can trust completely, and who will help you.

Six in the fifth place: You are failing to recognise someone who can be a great help to you. However, this person's true quality will soon become apparent to you. Once this happens, you are obliged to work with this person and accept this help without further mistrust.

Nine at the top: You are misjudging your situation and your friends. You thereby place yourself in defensive isolation. If you realise your folly in time, the situation will improve.

39

OBSTRUCTION: DIFFICULTIES AND IMMINENT DANGER

THE SCENARIO Here is trouble: an obstacle that must be overcome before you can go any further. This problem could be within yourself — an attitude, hope, or expectation that is blocking other possibilities in your life. The difficulty may be external. In any case, you must pause and build up strength. You should seek qualified help.

Despite the fact that you seem to be virtually surrounded by obstacles, this is nevertheless an excellent time for self-development. The value of obstacles is that we need to cultivate strength to overcome them. Difficulties foster strength: having things easy can make you weak. Thorough self-examination to determine exactly where the difficulty lies is recommended.

BUSINESS IMPLICATIONS There seems to be a blockage in the works which is adversely affecting the smooth operation of the business. Be advised that this difficulty is most probably an internal management problem. The blockage is based in staff or management attitudes. Call in outside help to assess your management procedures.

LOVE IMPLICATIONS Your relationship is facing a crisis, and there is every indication that you have caused it yourself through an attitude you have cultivated. The problem is actually inside you. You must first accept the fact that this problem is your responsibility: only by accepting this fact can you begin to work towards a resolution.

SPIRITUAL IMPLICATIONS You must accept full responsibility for your faults. Don't try to blame others for your mistakes and errors. Be introspective: this will be a source of inner enrichment and learning.

THE MOVING ELEMENTS IN THE SITUATION

Six at the beginning: When you strike a problem, you should stop and think about solutions rather than blindly blundering on. At present you should retreat slightly and wait patiently for the right moment to act: when there is a strong possibility of success.

Six in the second place: Normally, it is wise to try to find ways to avoid trouble — to follow the path of least resistance. However, on this occasion you are serving a cause, and it is your duty to meet the trouble head-on. This adds greatly to the difficulty of the situation, but there's nothing else you can do.

Nine in the third place: If you plunge yourself into a struggle now you needlessly endanger yourself, and jeopardise your security. Retreat, and the situation will resolve itself.

Six in the fourth place: You cannot manage the problem single-handedly. If you persist in the struggle alone you will fail. You must withdraw and organise some reliable assistance to attack the problem.

Nine in the fifth place: You are being called upon to help in an emergency. Don't try to back out. Roll up your sleeves and get on with it. You are the right person for the job. It will help to organise some assistance.

Six at the top: A problem exists that you'd rather ignore. Though it is tempting to turn your back, and carry on, this is not possible. Duty calls: you cannot ignore it. It will help to cultivate some competent allies.

40

DELIVERANCE, RELEASE FROM INDECISION

THE SCENARIO A period of indecision, anxiety and strife gives way to firm and aggressive action. Clear the air and resolve all the issues that have been troubling you. Be forgiving, bypass the knottier problems, and put the past behind you. The worst danger is over. All the problems have not been resolved yet, but now they can be tackled. If it is obvious that something could or should be done right now, get on with it.

Your luck is on the turn. Be magnanimous and forgive, so that in turn you will be forgiven. Do not dwell on the errors of the past. Make a new start.

BUSINESS IMPLICATIONS Recession is easing and you will soon be able to act with firmness and aggression. Get that new product into the marketplace. Put the past behind you. You must give staff members a second chance if they haven't always met expectations. Make firm decisions, and proceed. Anything is possible now — from expansions to mergers.

LOVE IMPLICATIONS Until now, your relationship has been in trouble. Large-scale misunderstandings and other difficulties have stood in the way of a fulfilling and satisfactory relationship. All this can now be resolved, and the relationship improved beyond all hope and expectation, with some effort on the part of both parties. The key ingredient here is forgiveness. You must forgive and forget each other's transgressions. Put them in the past. Resolve your conflicts, bypass problems and relieve the tension.

SPIRITUAL IMPLICATIONS When personal mistakes, errors or weaknesses come to light, the person on the spiritual path does not dwell on these negative aspects. If the errors or transgressions are unintentional, you should simply pass over them. We forgive misdeeds, for before we can forgive others, we must forgive ourselves. Forgiveness washes clean, like water.

THE MOVING ELEMENTS IN THE SITUATION

Six at the beginning: You have succeeded. Relax and consolidate. Recuperate in peace: the danger is past.

Nine in the second place: Some elements of the situation are out of your control. There are people around you, like self-serving 'yes-men' who are obstacles. Your only option is to be perfectly straightforward and honest. Don't become a 'yes-man' yourself.

Six in the third place: You are an upstart. You have risen quickly in the world, acquired money, and perhaps authority. However, you are managing these things very badly, and you will attract trouble and disaster.

Nine in the fourth place: Watch out for flatterers and false friends. If you allow yourself to become too attached to these sorts of people, you will not be able to join the worthy people, with whom you have inner connections, when the time for action arrives.

Six in the fifth place: Only you can save yourself. You must break off with all the inferior people and elements in your life, and refuse to be dependent upon them.

Six at the top: You have an enemy who is preventing your deliverance. Prepare to act forcefully. Make careful plans, and pay attention to the timing before you act.

41

DECREASE

THE SCENARIO This hexagram has an inner and an outer meaning. The outer meaning: this is a period of decline. Business reverses are inevitable and there is a general failure of expectations. You must accept this decline by simplifying your life. Luck does not shine for you, and you should take no chances at all. Anything that seems to show promise will have no satisfactory result. Try to control your anger and indignation at this turn of events. Avoid frustration by modifying your desires, so you will not be disappointed.

The inner meaning: you are undergoing a period of a sharp decrease in the activity of the lower faculties, or untutored instincts, and a corresponding increase in the activity of the higher life of the mind. You must cultivate simplicity and make sacrifices and this will lead you towards a higher life. Do not try to cover up inner poverty with empty pretence.

BUSINESS IMPLICATIONS Reverses are now inevitable. There isn't really very much you can do. This is a period of material decline. However, there is a possibility that by streamlining your operations, cutting back on staff and production levels, and achieving simplicity, you will benefit when the business cycle turns upwards again.

LOVE IMPLICATIONS In the outer meaning: this relationship is on the decline. What seemed so promising has proved to be infertile. You have failed to expect the unexpected, which is a common failure among those who like to make comprehensive plans. Perhaps it is better to drop the relationship.

The inner meaning suggests that as a couple you have been able to overcome the base instincts that can bring two people together — like lust and insecurity — and now there is opportunity for the higher attributes — unconditional love and respect — to gain more influence. This latter meaning is an optimistic outlook.

SPIRITUAL IMPLICATIONS You have a stubborn strength that might easily be changed into anger. Also, you have the human tendency to have an unchecked gaiety of heart that can develop into pure self-indulgence. Anger and desire are two things in your character that could stand to be decreased. By decreasing the lower powers of the psyche, the higher aspects of the spirit will be automatically enriched.

THE MOVING ELEMENTS IN THE SITUATION

Nine at the beginning: You have completed your own duties, and are now in a position to help someone else. This is fine, provided you don't brag about this or harm the other person with your assistance. Be wary of accepting help from others.

Nine in the second place: You wish to be of service to others. This is fine, but you must take care to retain your dignity and individuality.

Six in the third place: When people form in groups, conflict and splintering are inevitable. Close bonds are possible only between two parties. If you happen to be alone now, you will soon find a companion who will complement you.

Six in the fourth place: You need to suppress your bad habits and faults, as these are keeping away people who can help you. This suppression will be difficult, as your environment re-inforces your bad habits. However, make the effort: you'll be glad you did.

Six in the fifth place: Your fate is to succeed, and nothing can change this. Carry on without fear.

Nine at the top: You must now expand your goals so that you reach the cosmic ideal of sharing. Share your wealth with others, and work hard for the good of the community. Work not only for your personal advantage, but for the communal good.

42

INCREASE

THE SCENARIO This is the time to act. Many benefits are available. You can break old habits, for you have the strength to accomplish challenges. However, situations that do not require effort can be weakening experiences, while situations in which you face difficulty foster your strength. It is a time to serve idealistic ends. You can make important decisions and undertake new ventures.

Remember that this period will not last. The energy here is such that it will soon be spent, so you must use it while it is available.

BUSINESS IMPLICATIONS This is an excellent time to reform, and remove all the dead wood that may have accumulated. All the negative aspects or practices that might have crept into the conduct of your affairs can be reformed. Likewise, new products and services may be launched with expectation of success. You have the strength to take on stiff competition. It might help now to examine the business practices of others in your line of business. When you see innovation, it will pay you to imitate. Likewise, if you see glaring faults or mistakes elsewhere, make sure that you are not guilty of the same errors.

LOVE IMPLICATIONS It is possible for you to completely renew your relationship. You can do this by deliberately reducing the inferior elements that exist between you, and by enhancing the positive features. Therefore, cast out jealousy, suspicion, argumentativeness, selfishness and other negative aspects, and embrace unconditional love, generosity, unselfish embraces. Pursue the romantic ideal of love, for it is presently there to be captured.

SPIRITUAL IMPLICATIONS When you discover good things or high spiritual practices in other people you should imitate and adopt them. If you perceive bad or evil things in yourself, make the effort to get rid of these things. This is the way to improve yourself. Cultivation of the moral sense is one of the most important steps on the spiritual path.

THE MOVING ELEMENTS IN THE SITUATION

Nine at the beginning: You have the energy to undertake some great work. Proceed, remembering that this energy is a gift. Stay humble and selfless, and your luck will be very great.

Six in the second place: Good things happen when you are open to them and when you take the trouble to produce the necessary conditions for them to happen. Then luck occurs all by itself. Don't start to take your good fortune for granted, and refrain from being egotistic.

Six in the third place: The situation initially looks bad. Either you or someone close is suffering a misfortune. This positive time is so powerful that it will cause good to come from the misfortune, and you will benefit greatly.

Six in the fourth place: You need to be a mediator. Make certain you are reasonable, disinterested and fair.

Nine in the fifth place: Have a kind heart. True kindness does not look for merit or gratitude. Be kind, and you will certainly be rewarded.

Nine at the top: You are neglecting your duty and helping nobody. You are too abrupt, so nobody co-operates with you. If you don't change your methods, you shall soon find that you are isolated and open to criticism and attack from others.

43

☰ ☱

BREAKTHROUGH

THE SCENARIO A change in conditions is occurring and a breakthrough is possible. The image given is a swollen river that bursts its banks. It is a time of many possibilities. You must be resolute and determined: opposing forces can be confronted and defeated. The truth must be faced, whatever the danger. Fight corruption and inferior elements within yourself and in others. Make your intentions very clear so that misunderstandings are eliminated. Flex your muscles, show your strength. Compromise with evil or inferior elements is out of the question. However, violence and direct force are not advisable, as these only engender more violence. The best way to fight negativity and evil is to vigorously promote and reinforce the positive and the good.

BUSINESS IMPLICATIONS Here is a breakthrough, perhaps into a new marketplace, or, with new products, into a whole new area. You may find yourself in vigorous competition. The best way to conduct this battle is to be uncompromising in your honesty and integrity, no matter what tactic the competition stoops to. Do not engage the competition head-on. The way to win is to ignore the opposition, and pour all your energy into producing a top-quality product. The high quality and good value will be the weapons that win this little war for you.

LOVE IMPLICATIONS There has been an obstacle in your relationship, but it is now possible to achieve understanding and fulfilment. The truths of your relationship must be faced before the faults and problems can be combated. Conflict and quarrels will not help. The best way to overcome your faults is to energetically promote the opposite: be selfless, forgiving, giving, and unconditionally loving.

SPIRITUAL IMPLICATIONS Avoid self-satisfaction and the sin of pride. As a spiritual person, you must realise that it is wrong to accumulate riches for yourself without consideration of the needs and wants of others. Know that all gathering is inevitably followed by dispersion. Also, it is important to remain open and flexible, and receptive to impressions and criticism. Practise self-examination to keep negative influences to a minimum.

THE MOVING ELEMENTS IN THE SITUATION

Nine at the beginning: You are tempted, even inspired, to press forward, but the opposition is stronger than you imagine. You are not really up to a major endeavour. Reconsider, as unexpected setbacks at the very beginning can be disastrous.

Nine in the second place: Preparation and readiness are vital. Be very careful. Keep your wits about you. By keeping watchful you will keep trouble at bay. By being aware, you will protect yourself, succeed, and find security.

Nine in the third place: You are in a nasty situation, in which you are somehow allied with an inferior or evil person or force. For some reason, this is necessary just now. However, this inferior power could easily injure you. People will misunderstand and speak against you. Do not worry. Stay true to yourself and your principles: the situation will resolve itself.

Nine in the fourth place: You are trying hard to push ahead, but there are some major obstacles in the way. You must surrender your independence for the moment, and allow yourself to be led. You are very obstinate and wilful, and it is most unlikely that you will listen to this advice, in which case, nothing will go well for you.

Nine in the fifth place: Difficulties keep cropping up like weeds in a garden. Resolution, determination, and steady effort are required to keep these down. This may seem like a never-ending, impossible task, but do not allow yourself to be deflected.

Six at the top: There is great danger here. The problem is that this danger is not apparent. In fact, it seems as if you have won. Everything looks easy and straightforward. You are off guard, and some little seed of evil within you (some delusion or conceit) remains. Evil is very hard to eradicate. If allowed to flourish through complacency, the evil will develop into new forms and cause disaster.

44

TEMPTATION AND SEDUCTION

THE SCENARIO This is the hexagram of temptation. The *I Ching* uses an image of a strong woman who surrenders herself in order to gain power. This temptation should be resisted. You must avoid inferior people and situations, like easy romance and get-rich-quick schemes. You will be tempted, but the small delights on offer will invite disaster. If you are not very cautious, restrained, and disciplined, you will meet trouble.

There is, however, a complication in this scenario: sometimes we are tempted by things we really should embrace. Some people are destined to meet, join together, and become mutually dependent. In this case, the coming together will be free of cheapness, selfishness and dishonesty, and you may allow yourself to surrender to temptation.

BUSINESS IMPLICATIONS There is danger here. You are tempted by what appears to be a most attractive proposition. This offer could be coming from anywhere: from your business or elsewhere. The offer, whatever it is, must be refused. If you accept this offer, you'll regret it.

LOVE IMPLICATIONS Temptation is present. Desire rises strongly within you. The other party is more than willing. If you are female, be sure that there is no dishonesty or selfishness involved in the offer of love and coupling. If there is, the situation will end badly. If you are male, be warned that this very tempting woman is much stronger than you, and has motives that may not be immediately apparent. You might imagine that you can manage the situation: dally, then get away without paying the price, but you are mistaken.

SPIRITUAL IMPLICATIONS The temptations of earthly life. Material things and sex are very attractive. They don't seem to be all that bad on the face of it: in fact, most indulgences seem insignificant. However, don't imagine for a moment that you can dally with these things and not be affected. If you are not careful, and if you do not strictly avoid temptation, you will leave the spiritual path.

THE MOVING ELEMENTS IN THE SITUATION

Six at the beginning: There is an inferior aspect in your life: a habit, an ideal, a practice, or a person. Now you have the opportunity to limit the negative effects of the inferior influence. If you do not do this, this aspect will grow and be the cause of much trouble and regret.

Nine in the second place: The inferior element, or person, in your life should be kept under control not with violence or force, but with gentle cunning. Do not let this element develop, like a virus, to work evil elsewhere.

Nine in the third place: You are greatly tempted, but you must resist this evil influence. Consider your situation, and try to clearly see what is happening. This will be painful, but you'll be very sorry if you don't make the effort.

Nine in the fourth place: Even people whom you (rightly or wrongly) consider to be inferior have a place in the scheme of things. It will pay you to keep on the right side of these people, as you will need them sooner or later. Don't be aloof: maintain cordial contact.

Nine in the fifth place: You must be tolerant and hide your bright light under a bushel. Don't put on airs and graces to impress, as you don't need to depend on display in order to get things done. Your personal charisma makes everybody co-operate with you.

Nine at the top: You are tempted to manage inferior people and elements by pretending that they do not exist. You will probably be accused of pride and snobbery. However, since you are tending to become a recluse, this doesn't matter.

45

GATHERING TOGETHER, ASSEMBLY IN A GROUP

THE SCENARIO This hexagram signifies the formation of a community. You must strive to eliminate disharmony and disagreement, and aim to create strong bonding. Place emphasis on relationships. Sacrificing your selfish, narrow interests for the welfare of a group will result in extremely good fortune. The collective interest should be paramount over the individual interest.

There is a suggestion here of a sudden and unexpected danger. Be on your guard. There is no need for paranoia, but maintain a careful watchfulness.

Great things may be accomplished by collective moral force working towards a common goal.

BUSINESS IMPLICATIONS Mergers, with others who market similar products and services to your own, are strongly indicated here. Small-minded individuality is not appropriate here. You need to join a union or a collective, which may mean sacrificing some of your independence, but the possible gains are great. A complete and positive change in circumstances is possible.

LOVE IMPLICATIONS If you could drop your selfish attitudes and start to think of yourself as part of a collective of two, the situation would improve. Learn to sacrifice your self-interest for the interests of the relationship. This way of thinking will lead to strong bonding, harmony, happiness and good fortune.

SPIRITUAL IMPLICATIONS You should seek out like-minded people, in order to create a moral force that is all the greater for being collective. Only collective moral force has any chance of reshaping the world.

THE MOVING ELEMENTS IN THE SITUATION

Six at the beginning: You belong to a group, but you are hesitating, reluctant to make a commitment and to fully trust the group leader. Express these doubts, ask for help: your doubts will be dispelled.

Six in the second place: You are very attracted to a group or cause. The reason for this is that there are forces at work in the world that draw together people who belong together. Therefore, it is right and beneficial for you to allow yourself to be attracted.

Six in the third place: You want to join a closed group, but are being shut out and isolated. There is nothing to do but look elsewhere for union.

Nine in the fourth place: You are gathering with others to serve some high purpose or to achieve a lofty, worthwhile goal. You are being unselfish and your work will certainly be successful.

Nine in the fifth place: You seem to be the centre of a spontaneous movement or gathering. This gives you influence, but there are some about you who have undesirable motives. You can only manage such people by proving your selflessness and unwavering dedication to your higher aims.

Six at the top: You try to join somebody or a group, but your good intentions have been misunderstood and you are rejected. This makes you sad, but do not despair: you may yet be accepted.

46

PUSHING UPWARD, ASCENDING

THE SCENARIO Here is a big effort directed towards growth, like a young plant that pushes its way upwards into the light. Breakthroughs are possible now. You can advance: try for promotion. Some choices must be made as to how to use your talent, abilities and strengths wisely. Perhaps you need to seek new paths. This is a time for work and effort. You must set to work now, and your own efforts will bring you success. Remember this rule: you get further by modesty, perseverance and adaptability than violence or force. Adapting to obstacles is better than battering your way through. Be like a tree, which grows steadily, without haste and without pause. The total of all your small efforts will be something great.

BUSINESS IMPLICATIONS Now you may successfully break into new markets and launch new products. However, don't expect instant success. Think of your product as if it were a tree: it starts life as a tiny seed which, when properly nurtured, sprouts and begins to grow. You must, therefore, take the long view, and allow this rich source of success and revenue to grow and accumulate slowly.

LOVE IMPLICATIONS You are at the very beginning of an affair or a marriage that shows great promise. The love you share is a small, fragile thing, which should be nourished like a young sapling. Gradually you will together accumulate experience and a wealth of understanding.

Your relationship will grow into something majestic, which is greater than the sum of its parts.

SPIRITUAL IMPLICATIONS Your spiritual growth is like that of a tree. It is slow, continuous and non-violent. You accumulate all the small virtues of character, and so gain greatness of heart and spirit. One day you find that you are wise.

THE MOVING ELEMENTS IN THE SITUATION

Six at the beginning: You are at the very beginning of growth. Be aware that you can now begin major tasks.

Nine in the second place: You are an honest, energetic character, but you don't quite fit in, as you pay too little attention to the niceties of life. Despite this, you will succeed because of the quality of your character.

Nine in the third place: Make a big push. All obstacles will fall away and you may follow your road without fear or hesitation. Life won't always be this easy: profit from this period while it lasts.

Six in the fourth place: Significant success in your endeavour is near. Fame and fortune, the trappings of success, will be yours.

Six in the fifth place: Success has come as you have grown, but it's essential that you don't let this lead to conceit. Keep a sober head on your shoulders and don't try to skip any of the stages of growth. Continue your calm, steady progress.

Six at the top: You are driven by blind ambition. You are pushing indiscriminately ahead without re-evaluation. You will exhaust yourself to no avail. Try not to act on impulse, and bring planning and consistency into your behaviour.

47

≡≡

OPPRESSION, EXHAUSTION

THE SCENARIO This hexagram signifies adversity. You have
reached the end of one particular way. You are foolish to
try to carry on as if everything is normal. Drop the pretence
and seek out a new way. You can no longer influence
people. Nobody believes what you say, so it is better to
say nothing at all. The image in the *I Ching* is that of a
dried-up lake.

Remember that the end of one way, however painful,
negative and hopeless, can be regarded as the beginning of
a new way. If you allow your spirit to be wounded by
setbacks, you will certainly be disadvantaged. It is far better
to face this period of necessary change without pessimism
or negativity.

You must change direction, for you are flogging a dead
horse. Study your purpose, desires and goals. Be prepared
to take personal risks in creating a new future. If you do
not change, realise that the only other way to manage an
adverse fate is to accept it.

BUSINESS IMPLICATIONS You are on the verge of bankruptcy. Your product or service is no longer a viable
proposition in the current marketplace. You must close
operations and set to work identifying or creating a new
product. You can no longer continue as you are.

LOVE IMPLICATIONS Some adverse influences are affecting
your love life. Your relationship may be over. It may be
time to walk away in the hope of a brighter future with

another person. There seems to be little hope. Nothing you say is believed. Better, then, to say nothing, and go your own way and be as cheerful and optimistic as possible under the circumstances.

SPIRITUAL IMPLICATIONS You are under pressure. It is a very adverse time. Try to see these troubles as a test: when the spiritual person meets with adversity, he or she remains cheerful and optimistic, which helps to create a situation that will bring success. Your inner stability must be stronger than the mere vagaries of fate. You may bend, but you will never break.

THE MOVING ELEMENTS IN THE SITUATION

Six at the beginning: You are in trouble and your self-pity is making matters worse. You are allowing the trouble to depress you, and this makes the situation all the more hopeless. Snap out of it.

Nine in the second place: You are suffering from an inner exhaustion. You have all you need, but are bored. Things have come to you too easily. You need a challenge or a worthwhile cause to make your life stimulating and interesting again.

Six in the third place: You are restless and indecisive. You rely on unreliable things and feel oppressed when your ill-conceived ideas don't work. You make mountains out of molehills, and you are not getting your priorities right. You will soon regret your stupidity.

Nine in the fourth place: You are in a position to relieve the exhaustion and oppression of others. You hesitate, and find obstacles in your path. Also, you receive little or no help from your peers. However, do not be discouraged. Keep trying and matters will improve.

Nine in the fifth place: You wish to aid others, but you are frustrated and obstructed by red tape. Persevere and gradually the situation will improve.

Six at the top: The oppression that afflicts you is nearly at an end. Don't allow your recent experiences to hold you back. The time has arrived for decision and action without fear.

48

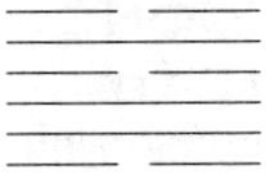

THE WELL, THE SOURCE OF NOURISHMENT

THE SCENARIO This hexagram symbolises the source of the collective truths that nourish humanity. This nourishing energy is always available, as it is an inexhaustible resource. You should be freely offering your advice, encouragement and assistance to any person who needs or asks for it. However, in order to tap this resource you need first to understand certain truths.

To succeed in any endeavour, you must mobilise all the necessary elements — appropriately directed energy, requisite skill and knowledge, and the correct equipment. If one element is missing, achievement is no longer possible.

When dealing with human institutions, like political or social organisations, it is essential that you understand the very foundations of life. Any superficial meddling will leave the deepest needs unsatisfied, the deepest roots unwatered.

In this situation there is a danger that you will fail to reach down to your deepest roots (the well of the divine) and remain fixed in convention, and therefore enslaved. You might find the effort of reaching to the depths too strenuous but if you do not persevere, you'll regret it.

BUSINESS IMPLICATIONS If you are unsuccessful, the reason is that one of the elements for success is missing from your equation. You need energy, skill and knowledge, and equipment, and these must be applied in the correct way.

LOVE IMPLICATIONS How is your relationship? If you

have been tapping the very deepest well of your nature, allowing the pure waters of unconditional love to flow unimpeded, you will be experiencing no problems in your relationship. If you have been behaving superficially, you will find that your deepest needs and desires are unsatisfied.

SPIRITUAL IMPLICATIONS Seek the universal truths. Bring forth the life within you by making the effort to reach the very deepest core of your inner self. Try to abandon conditioning and education, and all the elements that make a slave of you and bind you in illusion.

THE MOVING ELEMENTS IN THE SITUATION

Six at the beginning: You are wasting your life. You are attached to things superficial and inferior. Your insights and ideas are worthless. Should you continue in this manner you will be abandoned by others.

Nine in the second place: You possess good qualities and talents but you do nothing with them. As a result, they wither, you are overlooked and consequently mix with the wrong crowd. Once that happens you can no longer attempt anything worthwhile.

Nine in the third place: Something is being overlooked. A vital element for success is not being used. It may be that it is you who is being ignored, or it may be something in your life, like an opportunity, that is being overlooked. Rectify this, and good fortune will follow.

Six in the fourth place: You need to take the time to put your life in order. Perhaps you need to further your education or develop your skills. This might put you out of circulation for a while, but enhancing your powers and abilities will bring rewards later.

Nine in the fifth place: You are potentially wise. You possess certain knowledge. However, wisdom can only be realised through practice in everyday activity. Wisdom must be used; knowledge should be practised.

Six at the top: You are a great person. Your spring of love and wisdom is inexhaustible. The more you give, the more you have to give. You give dependable advice, share your experience and achieve exceptional fulfilment.

49

<u>≡≡</u>
≡ ≡
≡≡
≡ ≡

REVOLUTION

THE SCENARIO The snake sheds its old, restricting skin. Here you are in the process of breaking out of an old way that you have outgrown. This may be traumatic, since it is a conflict situation that opens the path to change, which you may feel quite nervous about as the change approaches. However, you will find confidence in the change even as it occurs. There is nothing to fear.

You need to mature, and here is the opportunity to do so. Learn the lessons of the past, and grasp this timely opportunity. Remember that the first law of the universe is change. Times change, and so do the demands on you. Get ready.

BUSINESS IMPLICATIONS Here is huge change — a revolution, in fact. Once this is accomplished, you will benefit greatly. In the meanwhile, you will require courage and bold management to implement the changes necessary. This is a vital stage in your company's evolution.

LOVE IMPLICATIONS Something in your life is about to change completely. If you are single, you can expect an end to this condition. If you are in a relationship, you are about to enter a new stage of maturity. Perhaps you have not been as devoted, sincere, and mature as you might have been until now: all this is about to change. You are going to break with the past and cast off all the old ways of doing things.

SPIRITUAL IMPLICATIONS Study the patterns of change

in nature. You are not separate from these changes. By tuning into them you can adjust your outlook and expectations so that they match the demands of different times. As usual, you must try to keep yourself free from selfish aims.

THE MOVING ELEMENTS IN THE SITUATION

Nine at the beginning: Don't be tempted to rush into change just because you don't have much else to do. Premature change will bring unfortunate results.

Six in the second place: You have tried to reform matters with no success, so revolution is necessary. You need to have a strong vision of the ultimate outcome and prepare your ground thoroughly. Seek competent assistance.

Nine in the third place: When making necessary changes you must avoid two errors. The first is to be impatient, aggressive, ruthless and unjust. The second is to be hesitant, conservative and timid. Seek a middle path. There is no need to change everything willy-nilly, but only those areas that have been a constant source of trouble and complaint.

Nine in the fourth place: You are faced with the possibility of radical and large-scale change. Whether this revolution will be successful depends upon you. You must question whether you are pushing these changes because of selfish, petty motives, or for some higher legitimate ones.

Nine in the fifth place: Trust your intuition in this matter. The signs of the impending changes are widely visible. Proceed: embrace the revolution.

Six at the top: Major changes have been accomplished, and now you must attend to minor details. Don't expect perfection or total victory. Look for satisfaction in what you have already achieved. Be happy with the attainable. If you continue to push matters you will be sorry.

50

THE COOKING POT

THE SCENARIO   This is an image of the preparation of food. In order to prepare nourishment, we need fire, water, food, and we must align these so that the fire burns steadily, the water heats and the food cooks. In our lives we must take similar care to prepare the ingredients necessary for success, and to bring them into harmony so that matters turn out as we would like.

Part of this process is the knowledge that there is nowhere on earth where the visible and invisible worlds do not intersect, and that the divine mainly manifests itself through humankind. In all our actions, we must be aware that what is visible and material actually has the capability of growing beyond itself to the realm of the invisible. That is to say, all human actions are imbued with spiritual implications. To live as if this is not the case is a mistake. You owe it to yourself to be aware of the invisible world and to nurture your invisible self.

BUSINESS IMPLICATIONS   This is usually regarded as a hexagram of material prosperity. You will do well, provided you are able to meet the needs of the marketplace.

LOVE IMPLICATIONS   Relationships exist on three levels: the physical, the intellectual and, perhaps most importantly, the spiritual. If you are in lust, you are successfully transacting on one level. If in time you do not open negotiations on the intellectual level, the relationship will end. The meeting of minds will help give duration to the physical relationship, but the only chance of permanence comes when the relationship extends to the spiritual level, and love becomes possible. You must consider your relationship in light of this. How many levels are you operating on?

SPIRITUAL IMPLICATIONS The will of the great spirit is revealed through holy people. If you are in the right place at the right time, correctly aligned with the force that brings power into a life, you may be one of these holy people. If so, it is a matter for humility and acquiescence to your fate.

THE MOVING ELEMENTS IN THE SITUATION

Six at the beginning: Every person of good will and intentions can succeed. No matter how inadequate you consider yourself, if you are honest you will succeed. You may need to use unorthodox methods but you should be able to prove yourself.

Nine in the second place: You are an outstanding personality, which naturally attracts envy. Don't allow that to be a problem. Concentrate on the job in hand.

Nine in the third place: You are talented but unrecognised, and this is a severe limitation. However, this situation may be your own fault. You should concentrate on adding a spiritual dimension to your abilities, which will make you more rounded. Then the situation should go your way.

Nine in the fourth place: You are not capable of doing your job, nor are you conscientious. You waste your time with inferior people. When limited expertise is coupled with grandiose plans, or weak character with responsibility, failure cannot be avoided.

Six in the fifth place: You are modest, receptive, highly approachable, and you attract the right people. Maintain this attitude, and you'll do well.

Nine at the top: You are a wise, good person. You give people help and advice in a spirit of mildness and unbiased compassion, which will bring benefits to you and all those fortunate enough to come into contact with you.

51

== ==
== ==
=====

AN AROUSING SHOCK

THE SCENARIO You have just had, or are about to have, a violent, sudden shock. You will be afraid, but this is a healthy reaction. Relief and laughter will follow this shock. Fear precedes reverence for the powers in the universe greater than yourself, and heralds a change for the better.

You have had a bad scare. Now examine your weaknesses, strengthen your character, and improve yourself. Only very special people would have not felt fear in the circumstances. These people are immune to outer terrors because of their stable inner self.

BUSINESS IMPLICATIONS You have just had, or are about to have, a thorough reorganisation of the business, followed by a change for the better. Innovative change is in the air. The initial difficulty signals a need to examine your weaknesses, so that by recognising them you can foster your strengths.

LOVE IMPLICATIONS You are in for a nasty shock and there is a likelihood that it is your fault. You may be unreasonably jealous or possessive, and are about to be revenged by your partner. Your relationship is in for a deserved shake-up, but there is nothing to worry about. As the shock recedes you will have the opportunity to experience a change in your attitude that will greatly improve your love life.

SPIRITUAL IMPLICATIONS If the shock didn't affect you, it means that you understand what fear really means. If the shock did affect you, set your life in order. Use the shock to examine and strengthen yourself. Search your heart to see that you do not harbour any secret opposition to the will of the universe or the great spirit.

THE MOVING ELEMENTS IN THE SITUATION

Nine at the beginning: A very unexpected event shocks and frightens you. You feel isolated and insecure. Yet, the very thing that frightened you will eventually turn out to be a source of good fortune.

Six in the second place: The shock endangers you personally and seems to cause great loss. Do not try to resist in any way. Remove yourself from the situation. Your losses are more apparent than real, and you will soon be in a position to recuperate.

Six in the third place: An external blow, a real stroke of fate, rocks you. Sometimes you can be so shaken by a heavy blow that you stop thinking. You will soon find a solution to the problem if you keep cool and maintain presence of mind.

Nine in the fourth place: You have been shocked into immobility by some terrible stroke of luck. You were unprepared for this, and are now confused. You must try to snap out of it.

Six in the fifth place: Here there is not one shock, but many. There is a constant stream of difficulties and strife. However, you do not lose your balance but weather the storm.

Six at the top: You have suffered a severe shock and are robbed for the moment of the ability to think clearly. You must keep still until your composure is restored. There is disaster all about you, and you have acquaintances embroiled in the strife, but you must withdraw as soon as you can. There is nothing you can do for anyone else.

52

A MOUNTAIN, KEEPING STILL

THE SCENARIO This is a time to quieten your heart. Some movement in your life has just come to an end and you have entered upon a stage of rest and stillness. Do not allow your thoughts to go beyond the basic requirements of your current situation. Focus on inner perspectives, and simply attend to the matters in hand. Being still will bring peace to your heart and give you peace of mind. Cease striving.

BUSINESS IMPLICATIONS Activity, like the launching of an aggressive market campaign, is not recommended at this time. Partnerships and mergers could easily fail. Be as still as possible, while concentrating on maintaining the status quo.

LOVE IMPLICATIONS Be aware that you have all you need in your current relationship. There is a real chance for peace in your heart and an end to restless searching. Sit back quietly and take serious stock of what you have. It is vital that you see things as they are. Keep your mind on the present situation. If you allow your imagination to wander, you will make your heart sore.

SPIRITUAL IMPLICATIONS Be still and calm. You must no longer seek tasks to do or ends to achieve. The end of work, ambition and longing is the beginning of other things. End your search for endings and beginnings, and in this way, find the widest beginning, the greatest end of all.

THE MOVING ELEMENTS IN THE SITUATION

Six at the beginning: You are calm. You instinctively see the situation as it is. You are at the very beginning of something, as yet unaffected by desires and interests that can obscure your best interests. Try to avoid selfish motives as you forge ahead.

Six in the second place: You are embroiled in a chain of events, and things are going wrong. However strong your desire to halt or change this process, there is nothing you can do but try to save yourself.

Nine in the third place: You want to be calm, but you are under pressure. Try some form of relaxation or meditation technique. Forcing matters will create more tension and endanger your health.

Six in the fourth place: The highest stage of rest, or keeping still, is the situation in which you forget your self (your ego). You are very close to this stage of self-mastery. Only your ego remains to be suppressed.

Six in the fifth place: You should always be very careful of what you say. You can easily say the wrong thing in dangerous situations. Always choose your words carefully. Avoid making unconsidered, thoughtless remarks. If you do so you will avoid a lot of unnecessary trouble and regret.

Nine at the top: When your inner composure embraces all aspects of your life and relationships, you are at rest and good fortune must result.

53

GRADUAL DEVELOPMENT, GRADUAL PROGRESS

THE SCENARIO This situation is like the slow development of a tree on a mountainside: growth proceeds slowly but surely. This is a time of slow and natural unfolding, and deliberate and careful cultivation.

The situation is like a properly organised marriage. There is no room for unseemly haste. There are various formalities to be taken care of. A gentle, penetrating and adaptable mien should reflect your inner calmness.

Even amid uncertainty, by you merely getting on with things, slowly but surely you can accomplish your purpose.

BUSINESS IMPLICATIONS Do not rush or force matters. You'll be sorry if you do. This is a time of slow, sure and natural growth. The possibility of beneficial mergers is indicated.

LOVE IMPLICATIONS You have met someone wonderful, whom you could love forever. This person is a fine marriage prospect. However, you must be careful to observe all the required niceties and formalities. Don't be in a heated rush. Take your time, like a butterfly drying its wings in the sun, moving with dignity and virtue.

SPIRITUAL IMPLICATIONS This is the hexagram of gradual awakening. No sudden or instant awakenings are lasting. True progress can only be gradual, and comes about because of constant personal effort.

THE MOVING ELEMENTS IN THE SITUATION

Six at the beginning: You are a lonely young person, just starting out in life. You are surrounded by problems and are naturally hesitant and slow. You are the subject of criticism, but it doesn't matter. You can benefit from the criticism, by using it to slowly lay the foundation for future success.

Six in the second place: You are developing. The initial insecurity of inexperience is overcome, and your first successes have been achieved. Try to share your good fortune with others, and this will bring you friendship and more good fortune.

Nine in the third place: You are moving too far, too fast, and you have lost your way. You have not let the situation develop gradually as it should but, rather, you have plunged yourself into a struggle. Therefore, you must stop trying to force the pace, and instead let things develop at their own pace.

Six in the fourth place: No matter how careful you are, you sometimes find yourself in an awkward predicament. You must exercise good sense and be flexible. Sidestep, yield, retreat: just do whatever it takes to keep trouble at bay.

Nine in the fifth place: There is malice and deceit at work here, which drives a wedge between you and your partner. It could be caused by someone close to you. The misunderstanding that has arisen will gradually pass, and truth will prevail.

Nine at the top: You are a success, and have become an example from which others may take inspiration.

54

THE MARRYING MAIDEN

THE SCENARIO This is a difficult situation, symbolised by an improper relationship between a headstrong young woman and an older man. A very great deal can go wrong in this time.

You should subordinate yourself. You could be searching for something in a place in which it does not and cannot exist. Propriety may be forgotten here. When you undertake something, it is important to know what to avoid as well as what to do.

You may not be able to restrain yourself: there is an intimation that desire long unfulfilled will burst wildly forth in any direction, in the way that raging floodwaters will burst the banks of a river at the weakest point. This means that you are in danger of losing control.

BUSINESS IMPLICATIONS Violations in standard business practice are occurring. A merger or partnership should be carefully scrutinised. This is not a time to be producing new products or trying to break into new markets. The most important element at present is knowing what exactly to avoid.

LOVE IMPLICATIONS Love is a voluntary relationship that depends in the long run on affection. Spontaneous affection between people is what binds them together. Without this the relationship is doomed to failure and sterility. If you are male, beware of a woman who only wants your money or position. If you are a woman, beware of a man who only seeks an outlet for lust.

SPIRITUAL IMPLICATIONS Life and love are fleeting things. However, the spiritual eye can discern the eternal in daily affairs. Keeping the eternal fixed in your mind brings benefits.

THE MOVING ELEMENTS IN THE SITUATION

Nine at the beginning: You are in a low position but have the confidence of someone in a high position. The best way you can have influence is by exercising tact, reserve and kindness.

Nine in the second place: You are faced with a disappointment, a failure of some sort. There is nothing for it but to persevere, alone if necessary.

Six in the third place: You suffer because you want things that you cannot have. To obtain luxuries that you cannot acquire honestly, you must compromise your morals and self-esteem.

Nine in the fourth place: You have talent and ability, but just now there are no opportunities for you. Do not throw yourself away on whatever is on offer: you will do better if you wait for the right opportunity to eventuate.

Six in the fifth place: You must forego vanity and pride. Even if you are placed in a socially superior position, try to be humble and modest.

Six at the top: You are going through the motions, preserving the socially acceptable form only. This situation is like a marriage of convenience, based on considerations other than love and mutual respect. This bodes no good.

55

ABUNDANCE, FULLNESS. THE ZENITH

THE SCENARIO This is a situation of full expansion or climax. Potential is fulfilled and all possibilities of further advancement have been exhausted. It is a time of extraordinary success and abundance. All you need, and all you have ever wanted is at hand. You should enjoy this peak of achievement as long as it lasts. You should put all outstanding disputes in your life to rest, meting out appropriate punishment or reward.

The important thing to recognise about this period is its brevity. It is a peak, a climax. After this, decline is inevitable, which is not a matter for regret or sadness, however, for it is just part of the natural cycle.

BUSINESS IMPLICATIONS You are at full expansion and have achieved market saturation. Therefore, do not invest further, but rather prepare for the natural decline in sales and productivity that is bound to follow this boom time.

LOVE IMPLICATIONS This is fulfilment. You have found someone who is everything you have ever wanted or needed in a partner. You are mature. That this climactic period may be followed by a physical decline should not be a cause of concern, as it is only natural. One of the few things that is exempt from the law of natural decline is human love.

SPIRITUAL IMPLICATIONS Be free of sorrow and care at this time of abundance and fulfilment. Embrace the coming decline for the heavenly process that it is.

THE MOVING ELEMENTS IN THE SITUATION

Nine at the beginning: You should be associating with people whose aims are similar to yours. Together you can bring about a period of prosperity. You have the necessary wisdom and knowledge. Now you need to find the energy.

Six in the second place: You are trying hard to get things done, but plots and intrigues delay and obscure your path. If you are forceful you will attract mistrust and envy, which will make the situation even more difficult. All you can do is gently persist, and be as honest and truthful as possible.

Nine in the third place: You are being hindered, and it is currently impossible to get much done.

Nine in the fourth place: You have the energy; all you need is the wisdom. In order to succeed, you only have to bring the right elements together.

Six in the fifth place: Be modest and invite advice from others. By accepting this advice you will bring fortune to everyone involved.

Six at the top: You are arrogant and obstinate and will achieve exactly the opposite of what you are striving for. You alienate everyone around you, and so are out of harmony. In the end you will be isolated and alone.

56

THE TRAVELLER (SEEKING A NEW WAY)

THE SCENARIO This is the image of a traveller. You may be on the road, in which case it is important to be humble and inconspicuous. You are alone in a strange place with no friends. Therefore, act humbly and be obliging towards others to avoid danger or unpleasantness. Avoid confrontation and keep moving.

You may not literally be a traveller on the road, but like all humanity, you are a traveller on a spiritual journey on the path of life. As you become aware of this, you should act the part of the traveller: be humble, and keep moving. Remember that long-term goals are unsuitable for the traveller. Do not be waylaid by protracted disputes; use your head, and keep on the move.

Remember, also, that the image of the traveller represents the lost soul or the restless person who mistakenly seeks to make changes within the self by embracing external change.

BUSINESS IMPLICATIONS Unless you are an itinerant merchant, this is a negative hexagram. The implication is that your current methods are somehow insufficient. Also, heed a warning of the dangers of involvement in lawsuits, which, if not managed expeditiously, tend to drag on at great expense to all concerned. You need to abandon current projects and preoccupations, and proceed with ever-changing market trends. Do not restrict yourself to any single product or service.

LOVE IMPLICATIONS You are only passing through. Make no long-term commitments. The wanderer has no fixed abode: home is the road. You can find friendship, and even sex, but love, with its need of commitment, seems out of reach.

SPIRITUAL IMPLICATIONS The world is a bridge, which we quickly cross. Build no houses or monuments. Take care to lodge only in suitable places. Earn your bread honestly, and associate with good people. In this way you will be able to travel your path unhindered, for only the lightest hearts are admitted to heaven.

THE MOVING ELEMENTS IN THE SITUATION

Six at the beginning: A wanderer is defenceless, but do not allow yourself to assume a demeaning role, hoping to earn friendship by playing the fool or the clown. Maintain a modest dignity. This will get you further in the end.

Six in the second place: You are behaving properly, being modest and reserved. People like you and in a new environment you can do well. Someone is ready to help you.

Nine in the third place: You are behaving very badly. You are meddling in matters that are none of your business. You are arrogant, and careless with people, and you will soon find yourself in the dangerous situation of being a stranger without friends.

Nine in the fourth place: You are a stranger in a strange land. You may have acquired property, but you can never be secure. Remember that material security is an illusion and, being a traveller, you should count on moving on sooner or later.

Six in the fifth place: Circumstances at times force the traveller to seek periodic work. If you are modest, generous and know how to behave, you can find friends and work, even in a foreign environment.

Nine at the top: You have forgotten that you are a humble traveller, which will lead to trouble. You are caught up in the karmic drama and you have lost sight of the reality of your existence as a wanderer, and consequently have lost your adaptability and modesty, which will result in misfortune.

57

≡≡
≡≡
≡———

GENTLE, PENETRATING INFLUENCE

THE SCENARIO This represents the gentle, yet penetrating, influence of human judgement. The application of calm, clear insight soon reveals and defeats all hidden motives that may be affecting you. You must act with clear insight, being gentle and proceeding gradually towards long-term goals. Conduct your affairs so this behaviour works to expand your destiny and advance your goals.

Ensure that things run smoothly. In this way you will not produce sudden, startling, spectacular results, but your progress will be more enduring and complete.

BUSINESS IMPLICATIONS Shun fast money. You must now adopt a very long-term outlook, and plan for a slow, but thorough, market saturation. Be sure that you understand how the marketplace operates. Then slowly work on your product or service. Remember that you are not trying for a quick success: you are working towards a gradual, sustainable, long-term success based on steady growth.

LOVE IMPLICATIONS This relationship cannot be described as 'love at first sight'. On the contrary, it must grow slowly like a plant in order to be successful. Consider what you want from this relationship. The person you are asking about is not to be trifled with. You will achieve satisfaction by taking a long-term view. If your motives are unworthy, you would do better to look for someone else, or change your attitude.

SPIRITUAL IMPLICATIONS If you wish to bring about permanent change within yourself, you must prepare thoroughly. Lasting change is only possible when you are ready to assimilate change. Do not look for sudden progress, which is counterproductive. The change you are seeking is not achieved by an act of will, but, rather, by gradual and unceasing effort.

THE MOVING ELEMENTS IN THE SITUATION

Six at the beginning: Do not be so gentle and gradual that you become indecisive. You must learn to stick to some goal, or you will simply drift and nothing will ever be resolved.

Nine in the second place: You have hidden enemies, or you are under the influence of some intangible, negative force that may be within yourself. This hidden trouble must be brought to light, for hidden enmity loses its power when exposed. The situation will have to be resolved before any progress can be made.

Nine in the third place: Don't think too long. Too much deliberation is procrastination. It is fine to think about things thoroughly, but you must also make a decision and act. The more you think, the more problems you imagine, and action will become impossible.

Six in the fourth place: The time has come for you to act with energy and decision. Use your experience and authority, and success is assured.

Nine in the fifth place: Reform is necessary. This requires careful planning, decisive action, and careful evaluation once the changes have taken place. Such care will ensure success.

Nine at the top: You are attempting to do too much, trying too hard. Taking on excessive activity drains your energy. Don't push so hard.

58

≡≡
≡≡

ENJOYMENT

THE SCENARIO This is the pleasant hexagram of friendliness and joy. Now is a time to encourage others to be expansive and to express themselves. Be kind, generous, and open to discussion and persuasion. Also, this is a period of opportunity for personal growth. Join friends, for knowledge is a refreshing and vitalising force that is most effective when shared. What you gain by friendship is far more secure and permanent than anything gained by force or intimidation. Almost anything you undertake at this time can succeed.

BUSINESS IMPLICATIONS The people who work in your business are that business's most valuable assets. Encourage them. Give them some access to the decision-making process. Allow them some creative input. You may be surprised at how productive a collective of minds can be.

LOVE IMPLICATIONS A lover should be, first of all, a respected friend. Here is an opportunity for friendship to develop into warm, passionate love. This will be a rewarding relationship for both parties.

SPIRITUAL IMPLICATIONS All knowledge, especially spiritual, should be a refreshing, stimulating, and revitalising influence. There is always something ponderous and one-sided about the learning of the self-educated. The best way to learn is through stimulating intercourse with others of like mind, with whom we practise the truths of life.

THE MOVING ELEMENTS IN THE SITUATION

Nine at the beginning: You are at rest and full of joy. You desire nothing. Your ego is still, and you experience true freedom, which is a state free of likes and dislikes.

Nine in the second place: You are mixing in the wrong company, and you feel tempted by inferior pleasures. You will find no satisfaction here. Strengthen your integrity, and do not be led. Do not squander your personal resources or waste your energy on base people or pleasures that you won't enjoy anyway.

Six in the third place: You are empty inside, and try to fill yourself with the pleasures of the flesh. Empty people need to be amused. Your pleasure-seeking is a symptom of a lack of inner stability, and spiritual emptiness. You will not be fulfilled in this manner. You will lose yourself.

Nine in the fourth place: You have a clear choice between positive and negative pleasures. You must choose, as you will have no peace until you do. You will be happy if you are able to recognise and embrace the higher path. If you choose the base path you will soon learn that base passions are a cause of suffering.

Nine in the fifth place: Even the best people can be tempted. You are leaning towards a corrupt, dangerous influence. If you allow yourself to have anything to do with such elements, you will be corrupted. Recognise the danger and protect yourself.

Six at the top: You have given up making decisions about your life. You are unstable, and you are simply swept along by events. You are a drifter, seduced by the base pleasures of the world.

59

≡≡

DISPERSION, DISSOLUTION

THE SCENARIO In this situation energy is being dispersed. There is a suggestion that your personal energy is working against resistance. In a higher sense, an obstacle that exists within every person is egotism. Our sense of self divides: it is the hardness and rigidity of the ego that causes many problems. One way to overcome this is to be dedicated to a collective purpose: religion can be useful here in dissolving the natural barriers between people. If you cannot accept the reality of the obstacle, you must cultivate a flexible attitude and approach. Try to look beyond ego limitations, to the wider and deeper moral and cosmic implications of the situation. Only a person free of selfish, ulterior motives can achieve this.

BUSINESS IMPLICATIONS This is an unfavourable indication for business, unless you are running an ashram. This is a time of ego-oriented competition. If your business is facing some sort of challenge, the only way to overcome it is to create within your workforce a sense of unity. Staff must pull together, with a common goal in mind. Otherwise, it's dog eat dog, and biggest pig wins.

LOVE IMPLICATIONS Your relationship is troubled by an obstacle to the free flow of love and good feelings. This is a result of egotism. Your ego is obstructing true communion. You will truly join when all selfish, ulterior motives between you are foresworn. This may be achieved gently and gradually.

SPIRITUAL IMPLICATIONS The ego is the biggest obstruction to spiritual advancement. Until you are able to
subdue this greedy, grasping part of the self you will remain
stuck firmly in illusion. It is difficult to dissolve the ego.
Only steadfast religious awe in the face of eternity and the
feeling of fellowship with all living creatures can do it. Keep
trying.

THE MOVING ELEMENTS IN THE SITUATION

Six at the beginning: You can see the problem quite clearly.
Although it is still small, it will soon cause misunderstanding and strife. Do something about it now. Nip it in the
bud.

Nine in the second place: Your problems come from within you.
You are impatient, unsympathetic, and alienated from
others. Get a grip on yourself. Fight to regain and maintain
a cheerful, optimistic outlook. Treat others with goodwill.
You'll regret it if you don't.

Six in the third place: Your task has become so great and so important that it requires a total effort and commitment,
which requires much self-sacrifice. This is the only way to
succeed.

Six in the fourth place: You must rise above party politics and leave
friendship out of this situation. This is the only way to get
anything done. Only very unusual people ever achieve a
wide view of the true interrelationships of life.

Nine in the fifth place: The situation is falling apart and the only
thing that will serve to reunite people is a great idea. This
will give people a common rallying point and help to pre-
serve and promote unity.

Nine at the top: Some deadly danger threatens, which you must
avoid any way you can. Duck! Dodge! Run away! Just get
you and yours clear. That is all that matters now.

60

LIMITATION

THE SCENARIO It is necessary to set limitations in your life. Economic limitations require thriftiness. Keep your spending within reasonable bounds. It is always wise to save something for times of scarcity. This means you should take steps to curb extremes.

Also, your personal life requires limitations. Without discrimination and the setting of limitations, your life would simply dissipate itself in the infinity of possibilities. Humans actually need limitations. You need duties and other limiting obligations that are freely accepted. Freedom only has significance in relation to its opposite: limitation.

You should evolve a system of limitations that suits you. This system should cover all aspects of your life: social, political, sexual, personal and professional.

BUSINESS IMPLICATIONS There may be hard times ahead. Make your business like a drought-resistant plant that has deep, abundant roots and minimal foliage. You must limit investment and expenditure. Avoid all excess. Do not undertake any radical reforms or ventures. Carefully regulate consumption and production with an eye for thrift.

LOVE IMPLICATIONS Even love must have limitations. You may love deeply and sincerely. Yet, there have to be limits. Do not be a spendthrift with your feelings and your devotion. To become and remain strong, certain limitations on your love must be set, and then voluntarily accepted. Otherwise, you risk losing your freedom of spirit.

SPIRITUAL IMPLICATIONS You will attain freedom as an individual seeker by accepting the limitations that morality, virtue and correct behaviour indicate, and by embracing them voluntarily. Only in this way will you be able to determine what your duty is.

THE MOVING ELEMENTS IN THE SITUATION

Nine at the beginning: You wish to do something, but you are confronted with many limitations. When you see obstacles you must not push on regardless. You should wait, and gather strength for another opportunity.

Nine in the second place: Here is an opportunity to act. Do not hesitate or procrastinate, because you will miss out. Proceed now.

Six in the third place: You are self-absorbed and dedicated to pleasure and enjoyment. This extravagance leads to a lack of restraint, and trouble lies ahead. Blaming others will not help you. Only the realisation that your troubles are your own fault will help.

Six in the fourth place: Some limitations are hard to stick to, but you are urged to accommodate yourself to them. If you can roll with the flow so that all your energy is applied to the matter in hand, you will benefit greatly.

Nine in the fifth place: Don't try to impose restrictions on other people without being prepared to set examples yourself or the result will be opposition and resentment.

Six at the top: Beware of being too severe when setting limits. Limits always provoke reaction and resentment. Nevertheless, there are occasions when severe limits need to be set. Sometimes, utter ruthlessness towards yourself is the only way to salvation.

61

INNER TRUTH, SINCERITY AND INWARD CONFIDENCE

THE SCENARIO You have an honest heart and mind, which is generally free of bias and, therefore, open to all manner of insight, for instance, that you have an 'inner' and an 'outer' self, and that when they connect it is possible to enter into new realities.

Try to be aware that there are realities that surround you. Be open and unbiased. Observe and accept. Now you can establish meaningful rapport with others and achieve a great deal by overcoming obstacles that have barred you in the past. You can also negotiate disputes. Your moral force can influence even obstinate, bigoted people.

BUSINESS IMPLICATIONS Major projects are possible now. You have a good product or service that you can believe in. You can even influence competitors.

LOVE IMPLICATIONS You are in love, and your love shines from your face like a beacon in the dark. Your love must be quite obvious to your beloved. Your unconditional acceptance of this person is an attractive force. A relationship that you cement now will be long, honest, happy and true.

SPIRITUAL IMPLICATIONS You must bring out the inner truth, which is not some relative thing that depends on circumstance or personality. This inner truth is reality, the truth that is universal and eternal.

THE MOVING ELEMENTS IN THE SITUATION

Nine at the beginning: The first step in cultivating truth is to be true to yourself, then to others. To be true, make sure you shun and avoid all form of intrigue. If you cease to be true to yourself, you cease to be your own person, and the inner power is lost.

Nine in the second place: Your insight and influence attract a friend. Your spiritual beauty awakens a response in others, and your influence will be more widespread than you can possibly imagine.

Six in the third place: You have no strength of your own: you rely too much on other people. Your moods are dictated by others. This may be the fate of those who love others deeply. You alternate between joy and sorrow. This is, depending on your point of view, the best or the worst aspect of love.

Six in the fourth place: You need to look outside yourself to find a higher goal and authority in order to elevate yourself beyond your current limitations. You must be humble and reverent, and shun worldly or selfish involvements.

Nine in the fifth place: You are in a position of leadership. Your job is to supply the basis of unity and harmony throughout your area of influence.

Nine at the top: Actions speak louder than words. Do not keep relying on mere words, for words cannot stand on their own. Example is still the best influence.

62

≡≡
≡≡
≡≡

THE PERSISTENCE OF THE SMALL OR WEAK

THE SCENARIO This time is for self-control and not for the implementation of new ideas. Do not persevere, or try to climb higher. Keep a low profile and consolidate. Conserve your resources and be patient: your time will come. The *I Ching* warns that exceptional modesty and conscientiousness are necessary, especially if you are a person of some authority. Be aware that great success is simply not possible in the circumstances. Remain frugal and conservative. Attend to detail and to small matters. Be sincere, unpretentious and simple.

BUSINESS IMPLICATIONS Times are not good. You must limit expenditure, conserve resources, and consolidate. Cultivate and maintain a low profile. Big programs of development or capital expenditure will have to wait.

LOVE IMPLICATIONS Small details are more important than major factors in the creation and maintenance of relationships. You must learn to be content with what is offering. It is inappropriate to aim for the glorious, all-consuming, classical passion. Love is often a quiet, ordinary, even humdrum thing. Its depth is revealed most in the tiny details of caring and consideration that a couple show to each other. Attend to these easily overlooked, day-to-day details that make up a loving relationship. Remember, too, the importance of honesty.

SPIRITUAL IMPLICATIONS The person on the spiritual path should be more conscientious than the ordinary person. Spiritual seekers should have their eyes fixed upon their purpose. Their actions are consequent: they are emotionally honest, simple and unpretentious. They give the fullest attention to the small details of life, allowing the larger truths to manifest in the small.

THE MOVING ELEMENTS IN THE SITUATION

Six at the beginning: You try to fly before your wings are ready. Forget your elaborate plans, and stick to the traditional and ordinary for the moment. Otherwise, you'll exhaust yourself and achieve nothing.

Six in the second place: Sometimes it is necessary to take unusual action. Normally, it is wise to go through the proper channels. However, in this case, in order to get into contact with superiors, or to get things done, you may need to use contacts, or deviate from the regular channels.

Nine in the third place: You are in danger. You may be in the right, but do not let self-confidence put you off-guard. There are dangers for people who are caught unawares. You can avoid trouble by expecting it.

Nine in the fourth place: Do not try to force the issue. Lie low and be humble. You'll regret it if you try to force a conclusion.

Six in the fifth place: Your strength is adequate for the task at hand, but you must be aware that you are in need of expert helpers, who will need to be recruited in a way that appeals to their sense of duty.

Six at the top: Your ambitions are too great. You do not know when to stop. Your aggressive actions will meet with disaster.

63

$$\equiv\!\equiv$$

AFTER COMPLETION

THE SCENARIO This is the end or climax of a phase in your life. The way peters out into chaos. Tie up loose ends, and attend to details as they arise. There may be a decline in material circumstances, but many of the negative effects of this phase can be alleviated by simply looking ahead and preparing for potential trouble before it occurs. If you feel depressed, remember that the end of one way is the beginning of another.

This hexagram also carries with it a warning that success is not without its dangers, and that what was once good fortune now becomes disorder as the old way of doing things disintegrates.

BUSINESS IMPLICATIONS This is a transitional phase. The run of a major product is at an end and the situation seems chaotic. It is vitally important that you ensure that all the little details that arise during this period are attended to promptly. Some planning should help to cushion any negative effects. Create a detailed contingency plan to manage possible difficulties now.

LOVE IMPLICATIONS The implication is that your relationship has reached some sort of resolution or climax. This may mean that it really is over, that separation is the next step, or that you have worked your way through the beginning stages of the relationship and are now ready to move on to the next stage.

SPIRITUAL IMPLICATIONS The situation seems to be

going reasonably well. This can sometimes create a sense of complacency, so that you are tempted to let things roll along, without troubling too much about detail. This complacency is a deadly enemy of the spiritual path. Only one who is always mindful and unremitting in care and attention is able to avoid error.

THE MOVING ELEMENTS IN THE SITUATION

Nine at the beginning: You are in danger of being caught up in a general rush. You must, however, slow down. Restrain your enthusiasm, or you will go too far and overreach yourself.

Six in the second place: You may feel very vulnerable, but you need have no fear. The possessions that truly belong to you cannot be lost. If you are patient and refrain from precipitant action, everything that seems to be lost will return to you.

Nine in the third place: You have a big plan, or you are facing an immense task. You can proceed, but you will never really win. This achievement will take a long time and the struggle will exhaust you. You should employ or work with only highly qualified people.

Six in the fourth place: Everything seems to be going very well, but elements of decay are at work. These evils may seem small and are easily ignored. However, they are omens that are neglected at your peril.

Nine in the fifth place: Don't bother trying to keep up with the Joneses, as it is a waste of time and energy. Place no value on ostentatious display. Sincerity and honesty count for more than appearances.

Six at the top: You may be tempted to pause and gloat over what has been achieved thus far. This is a mistake. You must put your shoulder to the wheel and not pause until the job in hand is done.

64

BEFORE COMPLETION

THE SCENARIO This represents the transition from chaos to order. A difficult time, you need to be wary, cautious and reserved. There is a warning against trying to take premature action. However, the general outlook is hopeful, for it is symbolised by the transition from winter's cold, barren stagnation to summer's warm, fruitful fertility.

Now the best thing you can do is take a long and careful look at yourself. What are you doing? Do you like the way your life is going? How does what you are doing relate to your long-term goals and purposes?

BUSINESS IMPLICATIONS The short-term outlook is bleak. It is possible to make expensive errors now. Do not undertake anything major. However, the long-term prospects are very favourable. Thus you should withdraw and prepare for the coming burst of opportunity and productivity.

LOVE IMPLICATIONS Do not push too hard or rush ahead. You may really like this person, but the feeling is not quite mutual yet. Play it cool, be wary and cautious and, above all, be patient. The long-term prospects for this relationship are excellent.

SPIRITUAL IMPLICATIONS The situation may seem to be going slowly. You feel that you are making little or no progress on the spiritual path. However, you are mistaken. You must maintain caution and reserve for progress to continue. Do not give up or relax, and refrain from becoming pessimistic. This winter of discontent will eventually evolve into the richness of summer.

THE MOVING ELEMENTS IN THE SITUATION

Six at the beginning: You are tempted to get busy, but you don't realise the implications of your situation or the consequences of precipitant action. Restrain your enthusiasm, for action now will bring on problems, failure, and even disgrace.

Nine in the second place: It is not yet time to act. That time will come, so you must prepare. Don't waste time in idleness: prepare to act when the time is right.

Six in the third place: It is time to act, but you are not well enough prepared, or strong enough to achieve your desires. To press on will result in frustration and failure. The only way to get ahead is to start all over again, perhaps in a different direction. Expert advice and professional assistance can help.

Nine in the fourth place: It is time to fight for what you want. This is a fight to the finish. Give no quarter. You must not hesitate or permit yourself the luxury of misgivings. The outcome of this struggle will lay the foundations of your future. If your enemy is visible and external, you are fortunate. The enemy can be internal and invisible: the forces of your own decadence.

Six in the fifth place: You have won. Honest determination and correct moral principles have brought you victory. Forget your misgivings, and put dread and worry aside. A new time is about to dawn, and good fortune will abound.

Nine at the top: You are on the threshold of a new phase in your life. This is a successful time, but you must be watchful of complacency and other dangers that success brings.

ALSO BY THIS AUTHOR

NEW AGE PALMISTRY
New Age Palmistry brings New Age awareness
and interpretations to centuries of traditional
knowledge of palmistry. Here is palmistry in
an innovative format that allows instant access
to this ancient science.

**YOUR LIFE IS IN THE PALM
OF YOUR HAND . . .**
Your hand is a map reflecting your personality,
your past and your personal potential. Fast
and accurate, this Portable Palmistry
Workshop is full of perceptive insight into our
deepest motivations and gives useful, practical
advice on managing work, family and
romantic relationships.

The approach is easy to understand, with
questions and answers. Even the novice can
begin reading palms immediately and with
confidence.

Includes notes on ● Reading your own hand
● The role of astrology ● Predicting the future
● Reflexology

OTHER NATURAL HEALTH TITLES FROM LOTHIAN

Judy Jacka
A-Z OF NATURAL THERAPIES
Here is a clear and simple reference for
anyone seeking information on how natural
therapies deal with a wide variety of illness,
and how professional therapists work.

Judy Jacka discusses symptoms, causes,
treatments and case histories to encourage an
understanding of a healthy body.

Also by Judy Jacka
FRONTIERS OF NATURAL THERAPIES
Among the traditional therapies,
acupuncture, chiropractic, herbal medicine,
homoeopathy, meditation and Tai Chi are but
a few of the many therapies now widely
practised in the Western world. Added to
them are exciting developments in our
understanding of the energy fields which are
related to bio-energetic medicine, vega-testing
and psychosomatics. These new approaches
to health all have the common goal of seeking
to promote a good life-style and to use natural
medicines and methods to improve health.
This book examines the principles and
practice behind all natural therapies and
wherever possible provides a scientific
framework for the concepts.

DOROTHY HALL'S HERBAL MEDICINE
This is the long awaited herbal by Dorothy
Hall, natural therapist and herbalist
extraordinary. She writes as only she can —
reflecting her years of research, her familiarity
with the plants, her clinical knowledge of the
physiological and other effects of herbal
treatments, and her unique perceptions and
understanding of the human character.

Dorothy Hall's is a new and fresh approach to
herbal medicine, discussing personality
analysis through herbs and demonstrating
how particular person-pictures can be built
up by looking at the person's needs for
particular herbs.